MARRIED LIFE AND
ITS VICISSITUDES

MARRIED LIFE AND ITS VICISSITUDES
A Therapeutic Approach

Arturo Varchevker

Routledge
Taylor & Francis Group
LONDON AND NEW YORK

First published 2016 by
Karnac Books Ltd.

Published 2018 by Routledge
2 Park Square, Milton Park, Abingdon, Oxon OX14 4RN
711 Third Avenue, New York, NY 10017, USA

Routledge is an imprint of the Taylor & Francis Group, an informa business

British Library Cataloguing in Publication Data

A C.I.P. for this book is available from the British Library

ISBN-13: 9781782203919 (pbk)

Typeset by Medlar Publishing Solutions Pvt Ltd, India

CONTENTS

ABOUT THE AUTHOR

Arturo Varchevker is a Fellow of the British Psychoanalytical Society, where he developed and chairs the Psychoanalytic Forum. He teaches in the UK and abroad, and his main area of interest in psychoanalysis is internal migration and psychic change. He is a marital and family therapist with a special interest in domestic violence and the impact of migration.

It gives me great pleasure to recommend this book by a very experienced couple psychotherapist. Arturo Varchevker is also a psychoanalyst, and it is particularly his long clinical experience with individuals, with couples, and with families that shines through. He is also trained in working systemically and in psychodrama, and the text gives abundant examples of his capacity to think about any situation from the perspectives of his different trainings, to try to find the most suitable angle from which to approach any particular problem, and then indeed to use these different disciplines together to think about and to treat his patients.

If the main enjoyment for the reader derives from the author's overall experience, there is one particular focus that is original, and of real interest to other clinicians and theoreticians, which is that of migration. This is obviously a topic which Varchevker has spent much time and imaginative energy contemplating, and, as well as being the particular theme of one of the chapters, it crops up regularly in virtually all the chapters as one of the central lenses Varchevker uses consistently to think about his patients and their dilemmas. He develops the idea that migration is a central part of any and every life, starting with the migration from womb to infant. In terms of couples, it is a fertile theme to ponder how becoming part of a couple for the first time is a major migration from a bodily individual unit to a two-body one, followed by moving between couple and individual states of mind, quite possibly followed by migration to engendering children and forming a family, and then all the migrations that form part of family life, of course including the geographical migration of more adult children away from their parents, and their parents needing to find a new form of being a couple again. All this as well as more literal migration, couples often being formed with one or both parties travelling to different lands and different cultures, and the real difficulties that inevitably ensue once an initial idealisation subsides and the partners have to learn how to live with each other—hopefully, lovingly, constructively, and creatively (the theme of another very interesting chapter)—in the real, unidealised everyday world of couple and family life. Personally, I found this perspective rewarding and very useful as an added way of thinking with regard to my own clinical work.

Arturo Varchevker's writing constantly manifests his grounding in Kleinian psychoanalysis. He was one of the editors of *In Pursuit of Psychic Change: The Betty Joseph Workshop*, and his writing reflects his immersion in some of the most creative contemporary Kleinian thinking, particularly the work of Ronald Britton, whose ideas are often quoted and then developed fruitfully within the couple frame.

What also comes across is Varchevker's capacity for forming sympathetic identifications with his patients. One feels that he feels what they feel, including his ability to stay with very difficult and uncomfortable feelings, for example of helplessness or torment. One can easily imagine that couples seeing him would often be helped simply by this quality of empathy: this is not particularly discussed in the text, but it emanates from it.

So, I hope readers will enjoy their reading journey, as I have, in the company of a distinguished and experienced clinician. This is an important book from which all couple clinicians will want to benefit. It will also illuminate many emotional dilemmas from a couple perspective, which other clinicians, whether working with individuals or families, will appreciate, as will the interested reader—it is one of Varchevker's strengths that his text is easy to read, unencumbered by jargon.

Francis Grier
September 2015

INTRODUCTION

The idea behind this book about couples and marital therapy came to my mind when I stopped working at the Marlborough Family Service, an institution I had been involved with for almost forty years. In addition to my psychoanalytic work, my experience with families and couples occupied a considerable portion of my time. I felt it would be a form of neglect not to leave some record of this experience and offer some ideas. To change, or not to change, or to resist change, is part of human nature. From birth onwards we can say that every emotional development incorporates some form of learning. Learning implies that there is a capacity to deal with losses. In this book I want to focus on a particular type of change and resistance to, or difficulties with, change that manifests itself in the therapeutic relationship and quite often becomes a handicap to a constructive therapeutic development or constructive change.

The title that I have chosen for this book is intended to indicate the complexities of married life: what may bring couples together and what may cause couples to seek marital help.

It is impossible to conceive of the individual in isolation while you read this book: an interaction takes place between what I have written and how you perceive it and understand it. The book aims to give a view of the complexity and subtlety of the different theoretical models and techniques in dealing with some of the most significant issues and problems presented by couples and my way of dealing with them.

From a temporal perspective, we can notice that the marital relationship can, in relation to the present, highlight enjoyment, security, and a sense of achievement, or it can activate anxieties, crisis, and a sense of disaster. In relation to the future, it may bring about the promise of hope; and as for the past, it usually filters through into the present, it can colour the future and can also activate positive past emotional experiences or it can activate dreaded past emotional experiences that colour the present interaction. Family culture and social culture can also influence all these different possibilities.

The marital relationship is an important unit within society. It lies in the middle of the individual and the family and activates a variety of interactions that range from what is positive, constructive, or enjoyable to the opposite, what is negative, destructive, and dreaded. This relationship can involve a genuine wish to be with a person with whom a good and constructive future is going to develop, or it can, instead, be an expression of the desire to be with someone in order to carry what that person does not want to or cannot own. The marital relationship can be a way of growing up and reaching the next step in an individual's development or it can operate as a block to development.

Each partner's emotional development, in terms of psychic and biological changes and the expected and unexpected vicissitudes of life, is likely to manifest in different ways in their interaction. I have mentioned in other publications the importance of taking into consideration the life cycle. For instance, young couples, adult couples, or couples that reach older age may present a similar type of interaction or symptoms but sometimes the meaning may vary at different stages of the life cycle. Another important aspect in marital relationships is the narcissism of both partners. This may pose a significant challenge in an active pathological narcissism, in contrast to a more normal or a healthy narcissism.

Montaigne famously wrote: "A good marriage would be between a blind wife and a deaf husband." In other words, the wife and husband know each other so well that they do not need to hear or see each other. However, when we approach the exploration of the couple and marriage, we are entering a very complex phenomenon. Sometimes a family therapist, after seeing the whole family together, may decide to focus the therapeutic work on the parents without their children. In other situations, the intensity of the marital relationship and the couple's crisis can distance the psychoanalytic patient from psychoanalytic intervention. At the same time, the boundaries or differentiation between individual, marital, and family approaches may be unclear, and the path may be indicated by the different needs of patients and the expectations and orientation of the therapist. However, when one of the partners presents a very disturbed psychotic personality, it is essential to request a psychiatric assessment.

According to Asen (1995), "Love can be a force for good or a force for evil". The couple has a vital importance in the psychological development of the individual and the family, and throughout the entire individual and family life cycle the presence and influence of love are manifested at both the conscious and the unconscious level.

Individuals experience a wish, a desire, or a need to establish a close, stable, intimate relationship with another person with whom they would like to share aspects of their lives, have new experiences, and construct a future. Relations between partners reflect the question of romance, intimacy, and desires, as well as how they will deal with equality and inequality and with their conscious and unconscious needs. It is an important relationship from the individual, family, and social perspective, and its complexity is enormous.

Sometimes we observe an intense need, mixed with eagerness and excitement, to establish a marital relationship; conversely, at other times we are confronted with the opposite reaction, either just before the couple relationship is out in the open, or when it is out of sight. The desire either to establish a marital relationship or to run away may depend on the emotional difficulties experienced by an individual. Each current or prospective partner's emotional interactions are informed by his or her early conceptions and misconceptions, especially in the sexual domain and around his or her oedipal experiences: these will, in turn, play a significant role in any possible future relationship. Early emotional histories, achievements, earlier traumas, family values, and culture are some of the additional factors that are likely to colour individuals' attitudes, either subtly or in an obvious way. Marriage is therefore a complex phenomenon that will play an important role in terms of expectations and pressures that will affect partners at both a conscious and an unconscious level.

Migration is a useful term to describe the process of integration and assimilation of new partners. There are conscious reasons and unconscious fantasies that cause people to migrate from being single to becoming a couple and developing a long-lasting relationship. Sometimes the loving attraction hides different levels of conflict related to varying personal circumstances, identities, and expectations, which activate a considerable amount of stress and conflict in marital partners, as well as in their families and their communities. Generally, couples and marriages share intimacy, goals, positive and negative experiences, difficulties, and conflicts through their interaction. For instance, intimacy implies closeness, mutuality, openness towards each other, the possibility of permanence, and the expression of love. But the external pressures of modern life, in terms of time, space, and technology, can interfere with this development, along with other external and internal pressures that can hinder the expression of intimacy.

In general, a couple or marital relationship refers to two individuals who have established a particular bond through living together or spending a great part of their time together and who share some degree of intimacy and sexuality and some form of future.

From a psychoanalytic perspective I consider that the individual is expected to develop in order to deal with emotional and biological changes and external needs and pressures. The life cycle allows the exploration of the individual's present situation in terms of the present emotional state, which also includes the external and internal pressures coming from families, friends, and socio-cultural contexts and the historical emotional development at a conscious and unconscious level. This manifests in different ways at different stages of the life cycle and can be activated within the transference situation.

The early years, and early emotional development, in terms of attachment and separation, are especially important in relation to future developments. How they are worked through will affect future developmental stages and conflicts. I consider the approach developed by Melanie Klein and her followers essential to understanding the present and the past emotional interactions of each individual. I also consider it important to explore the different ethnic, cultural, social, and gender contexts that have an effect on the various phases of the life cycle. It is important to be aware of these contexts and their effect on the patient and on the therapist.

The theory of the Oedipus complex was developed by Freud, who considered it central to exploring and understanding the mind's functioning. I want to underline the importance of exploring the variations of the Oedipus complex at different stages of the life cycle and how they can impact on the marital relationship.

It is well-known that emotional difficulties or trauma in early childhood tend to be reactivated and affect the individual's capacity to work through stresses that may appear at later stages of the life cycle. As I mentioned above, it is important to locate the stage of the life cycle at which the individual is experiencing considerable anxieties or stress due to some form of migration or trauma, because the meaning of what is happening and how it is happening can be significantly different at different stages of the life cycle.

Each stage confronts the individual with significant changes and often activates stress and anxiety. In essence, these stresses refer to conscious or unconscious awareness about the individual's own life, in terms of biological, emotional, and interactive situations. Of course, there are external situations in life, and some quite stressful ones, and all of them can reactivate oedipal anxieties in a very intense way.

As Freud, and philosophers, and writers before him have said, it is impossible to conceive of the human being in isolation. The pronoun "I" implies that there is "another". The individual does not exist in isolation: from the moment the baby is able to recognise and acknowledge another object or the other, there is always a relationship. This very early object relationship is going to affect both parties in their interaction, but it is the baby who is going to be especially affected. Introjections of a good containing experience are extremely important, because they help the baby to deal with the innate conflict of love and hate.

The first human relationship is established between the baby and its mother and, from this perspective, coming out of the womb is the first migration. How this relationship was established and how it has developed is going to have an influence on the capacity to develop individually, in relationships, and, of course, in the couple relationship. Thus, getting married is another form of migration.

At the same time we can also view the couple as the social axis that connects the individual with himself or herself and the outer world—parents, siblings, family, and society. These are very important conceptualisations that highlight aspects of the human mind. Emotional outbursts and derailments at the individual, marital, family, and society level affect us in many different ways. This broad view highlights the multiplicity and complexity of the issue we are addressing.

Within the psychoanalytic perspective, Freud made use of the Oedipus myth to explore and understand a fundamental aspect of the interaction of individuals. Couple and family therapists have recognised the centrality of this myth to understand the possible developments of the individual within the couple and the couple within the family, and vice versa.

The myth begins with the pairing of Laius and Jocasta, King and Queen of Thebes. The crisis began with the birth of Oedipus—a passage from there being two people to three. Freud located the Oedipus complex as operating from the age of three years onwards. Melanie Klein was able to confirm and explore this phenomenon from the perspective she gained by working with children and watching their games, recreating the peculiarities already described by Freud. She found, from a developmental perspective, that the Oedipus complex starts earlier than anticipated by Freud; at the same time, she emphasised the importance of what she called "the oedipal situation".

Ron Britton, basing his ideas on Melanie Klein's (1975) contributions on the early Oedipus complex and on Bion's (1970) concept of container and contained, describes how the infant is activated by his curiosity, which leads him to recognise that a relationship exists between his parents that is independent of him. Britton (1989) describes this third position as fundamental to the ability to produce the Oedipus complex, where being excluded from the couple brings about the exclusion from the mother–father relationship. The ability to tolerate and develop this exclusion brings with it the possibility of recognising oneself as someone separate: in this way, intersubjectivity is associated with an appreciation of the partner. Failure in this development brings with it the difficulty of recognising the partner's space. The important issue is the difficulty of dealing with situations of loss. Catastrophic anxieties often acquire an intensity that threatens the psychic equilibrium of the marital relationship.

In relation to marital therapy, my impression is that most marital therapists have done their basic training in psychoanalysis, psychodynamic psychotherapy, behaviour therapy, family systems, or psychodrama. So far, there have been comparatively few, limited courses in marital therapy, in contrast to the large and growing number of marital problems and divorces.

It is possible to consider that the steep increase in divorce is linked to social and cultural changes and is therefore about something significantly different from that which takes place in traditional marriages and families. These changes manifest in the lifestyle of individuals and families in Western culture, and are, of course, more noticeable in large cities. The traditional type of marriage is maintained to a considerable degree in small villages and in other cultures, and also within strong religious practices.

The rapid growth of technological development has brought with it hope for some form of egalitarian relationship between men and women. This can often become a source of open or hidden conflict within marital relationships, because men and women enter into them with significantly different role expectations and personal histories. A woman who has been used to traditional marriage in her family of origin, for instance, might long for an egalitarian relationship with her spouse, but, when they get together, this hope may clash with her own sense of affiliation to her own family and become a source of conscious or unconscious emotional conflict. Or her expectations may arouse an antagonistic attitude in her partner. The same can develop in the man, in the opposite direction.

In relation to this, important questions are: When does a couple become a couple? What is a couple? Are two individuals able to share the emotions activated by their past and present situations? Are they able to develop intimate domestic lives? Or is it a way of basically negotiating and sharing their respective individual, family, and community hopes and fears? Sometimes these types of relationships are supported by different interactive pressures, and there is a need on the part of each partner, at a conscious and unconscious level, for a necessary containment that allows a positive negotiation between them. In addition, there is the possibility of considerable pressure coming from external contexts, such as their own families of origin, culture, and society, and this may affect either their decision to enter into a couple or marital relationship or their interactions.

The technological developments of recent decades have brought about significant social and cultural changes: for instance, in Western urban society there has been a significant increase in the number of nuclear families that are quite different from those traditional extended families in which support and control is provided for children, adolescents, and young adults. Nuclear families often foster a sense of independence in young adults, encouraging them to stand on their own two feet and earn their own living, activating in many of them a sense of autonomy and the wish to enter into a marital relationship.

Significantly varied cultural patterns in marital couples also exist outside the big cities of the Western world. There are religious families, who establish strong rules about whom their children should marry and how their marriage should develop. Another feature of our times is that middle-class families foster and welcome their sons and daughters marrying someone from the same social class, or somewhat higher. Lower-class families seem to have less influence on their children. In every social class and culture we observe the effect of early parenthood on children and on their development. All this is likely to have an effect on the couple's choice and the development of the relationship.

The general expectation is that in the couple or marital relationship the partners will be able to develop and share intimacy and some plans for the future; in some cases, this includes becoming a family. Attraction and love are among the most important ingredients for developing a good marital relationship. In the past, love was associated with eternity, in terms of "I will love you forever." Nowadays, this view has changed, and other types of attitude have been activated, where attraction and love are linked to the existing individual, social, and cultural expectations.

At the same time, this dyadic relationship develops specific characteristics, as the partners have different—or similar—internal and external circumstances. Each has developed a personality and future expectations, in addition to the way their own respective families have influenced them at a conscious or unconscious level.

Following the socio-cultural frame in Western culture, and in other cultures as well, the man is seen as the one with power in couple and family relations. "Macho" is a Spanish word that portrays this meaning. The man is seen as sexually potent, successful, and independent, the woman as weak, dependent—the one who cries and feels insecure. This can create a type of interaction in which both members are happy with the situation and, following this view, can develop their own features. The feminist movement has opposed this concept and fought against it, though some women have partly identified with their antagonists, who put them down. Sometimes men and women try to achieve a more egalitarian outcome.

The couple's identity is connected with issues of prejudice and ethnic values. This refers to actions or estimations about preferences and the importance that we ascribe to some influential contexts at a social, family, and personal level: to things, situations, culture, ideologies, ideas, people, spirituality, and religion. In Western society, the emphasis is on individuality and freedom. Within this perspective, there is a wish to see people asserting their freedom. In order for that to occur, we activate the capacity for introspection: empathic understanding flows with greater ease in those who share the same cultural background.

As described above, each partner has his or her own personality and identity, and this allows them to enter into the couple or marital relationship in a full sense, in terms of taking part in a positive interaction or the opposite. I have observed another type of interaction in some couples who maintain a distance from each other, where one or both members assert their identity and independence. This can activate different types of destructive interactions and can often lead to an intense symmetrical crisis that at times can feel overwhelming.

I also want to mention another phenomenon that has grown in recent decades: the migration of people between countries and continents, which has been responsible for the coming together on an unprecedented scale of couples from different cultural and racial backgrounds. So far I have been using the concept of external migration to describe external changes and physical developments, and internal migration to describe the psychological manifestations brought about by these changes.

In relation to migration from one country to another or marrying a partner from another country or another culture, it is important to understand the significance of the role played by ethnicity in shaping our thinking, feeling, and behaviour; the way we establish patterns of behaviour, keep rituals alive, how we eat, talk, celebrate, and deal with everyday matters as well as important events of our lives. Monica McGoldrick (1998) equates the concept of ethnicity with "peoplehood": a combination of race, religion, history, myths, language, and more. It is a combination of conscious and unconscious processes where all these aspects, at different levels, are interwoven within the development of each individual. It contributes to the development of a sense of identity and historical continuity, securing a sense of affiliation to the family, to the community, to those who share a common set of values and history, real or fictitious. The concept of values denotes the priority that each partner ascribes to himself or herself; it is often influenced by social background, family, and personal relationships. These values must be integrated into the marital relationship or denied or rejected.

For a successful interaction to occur, it is necessary to activate the capacity for introspection and empathic understanding. This flows with greater ease in those who share the same cultural background. The wish or need for power—whether used in a constructive or a destructive way—does, of course, have a significant effect on most situations. This applies to individuals, couples, families, institutions, political parties. It is also present in any therapeutic relationship. People can use it, accommodate to it, or resist it.

The marital relationship is the basic socio-cultural unit between the individual and the family, and the interaction between the two is affected, as I have mentioned, by many pressures from within and from without. Problems and conflicts are part of the day-to-day interaction of most marital couples. Some problems are an indication of a serious disturbance and may have a pathological origin outside the marriage. In the various chapters in this book, I have grouped relevant and familiar topics in order to examine and understand the possible dynamics within different marital situations. I have chosen a range of significant topics that can provide a clear understanding of the different marital relationships, their potential problems and their psychopathology at different stages of the life cycle. From the therapeutic perspective, I hope this book will make a significant contribution that might facilitate the understanding of marital vicissitudes and a constructive development of marital relationships, and be applied in marital therapy.

CHAPTER ONE

Similarities and differences in marital relationships

Similarities and differences are the basic ingredients in any relationship. They contribute to positive development as well as to emotional disturbances. There are positive similarities and negative similarities. Usually, failure to deal with them has a destructive effect not only on individuals, marital couples, families, professionals, or institutions, but also on society in general.

The history of humankind provides many examples of the difficulties in accepting sameness and tolerating and integrating differences. It would seem that most wars have been fuelled by this basic conflict. In relation to society, we are now confronted with the phenomena of globalisation, lack of financial resources, and economic crisis. The well-known principles of equality and democracy are presented in a seductive way but lack consistency. Issues of identity, power, loss, and uncertainty are some of the main causes of anxiety in individuals, couples, families, and institutions. We can explore these issues in relation to the history of humanity, and we can also look at our present situation and the different types of external and internal pressures.

Unfortunately, dependency exposes the weak to being abused or exploited by the strong or the powerful. At the same time, it is important not to lose awareness that this gloomy picture of the human condition, which is very familiar, is not the totality of what is happening. On some occasions, humans also have the possibility of developing positive, constructive, creative attitudes, even in very difficult circumstances.

As an introduction to this subject, I want to draw the reader's attention to an ongoing debate in the field of psychotherapy: that concerning history versus structure. The relationship between these two approaches has been an area of investigation, reflection, and debate among psychoanalysts and systemic therapists in their respective fields. The narrative approach focuses on historical aspects, and the relational approach focuses on the structural perspective. The latter refers to the notion of space, dimension, and order or links within the structure, whereas history has to do with temporality and all the possible changes that develop within the notion of time, in terms of past, present, and future. The two approaches are interrelated, because changes within the structure are affected or accounted for by the notion of time and therefore of history. Narrative takes place within the mind and describes events or impressions from the past; at the same time, it is addressed to another person, group, or audience. Within this viewpoint, we can observe an interaction that activates both aspects. Mental or psychological structures are likely to be affected by what has developed in the past, is developing now, and may develop in the future, in reality or in fantasy.

In this chapter I first explore similarities and differences at an individual level from a psychoanalytic angle, taking into consideration a developmental perspective. Then I focus on similarities and differences at a marital level, bringing together a psychoanalytic and systemic view. In relation to similarities and differences, one suggests monotony, the other suggests variation. Similarities and differences can promote constructive development, and it is important to explore and understand the way this functions.

Similarities and differences at an individual level

Psychoanalysis has shown how perceptions of the other are misconstrued through our own projections. Studying the emotional life of infants, one can easily see the vulnerability of the infant, who often develops extreme emotional reactions as a coping mechanism. These extreme emotions can turn the infant into a little dictator or a panicky "desperado". The temporary absence of an object can be experienced as total disappearance. Mother has gone for ever. Appearance and disappearance follow the rules of magic and omnipotence in the fantasy world of the baby. The baby's initial perceptions centre on his relation to the mother-breast. Extreme dependency, gratification, and frustration are hallmarks of this relationship. At the initial stages of development, the baby struggles to deal with the faults and imperfections of his mother or immediate carers. The baby copes with this by separating a perception of his mother (breast, bottle, etc.) as entirely good and perfect from the frustrating experience (absent mother, etc.). At the very early stages of the baby's development, he does this because he has not reached a stage of development that allows him to have reached that recognition. Later on, the baby turns to this form of perceptual splitting in order to cope with the intense emotions aroused by this experience. We need to remind ourselves that for the baby the frustrations and gratifications acquire an overwhelming quality, as can be seen by observing the effect on the mother of the persistent or desperate crying of her baby. We infer that the baby finds it emotionally difficult to integrate these two opposing experiences as belonging to the same breast or mother. To be able to emotionally negotiate these perceptions is important: Melanie Klein referred to it as achieving the "depressive position". This is the basic experience of coping with difference, in terms of recognising that it is the same object that has been perceived as good when gratifying the baby and as bad when the baby was hungry and felt frustrated.

I said above that at the very beginning it was not possible to achieve this position because of biological immaturity; now I am referring to emotional immaturity. Emotional immaturity is a loaded term with moralistic overtones and is difficult to evaluate. Through detailed observations of babies and clinical work with children and adult patients, it is inferred that their way of dealing with their past situation can highlight and foster good emotional development, which will shape a healthy personality, or the opposite, in terms of weakness and pathology. For instance, the need to preserve the good experience or the good bond with the mother may require that the baby enhance in phantasy the qualities of the mother, so the good experience is magnified and idealised and the bad or frustrating experience is minimised, leading to the phenomena of idealisation and denigration and to persecution, which, in turn, result in a tendency to perceive people and experiences in radically opposite ways. Seeing the bases of this type of phenomenon is very important in understanding the problems of racism and violence—for instance, where all qualities of purity, perfection, and greatness were attributed to the Nazi motherland, and everything that was evil, subhuman, and contaminated was attributed to Jews by a mechanism of projection and denial of what had been projected. In psychoanalysis, this form of mental process is called projective identification: a part of the self that is unwanted is got rid of, split off, and perceived in someone else and not recognised as belonging to the subject.

Thinking about similarities and differences brings to mind an experience I had when I was staying in a village in a valley in Switzerland. Someone had died, and I realised that people from the village and from outside were coming to pay their respects. I enquired who had died, and the person I asked replied, "She wasn't from here, she didn't belong to the village." "Oh! Was she a visitor?" "No, she lived here." How long did she live in this village? "She lived here for over fifteen years. She had come from another village and got married here." How far away was her village? "Ten kilometres"! This example highlights how people deal with similarities and differences; something that is of paramount importance in any form of human interaction, whether in a marital, family, or social situation.

"Sameness" implies a comparison, the presence of another person or thing; to say "John is like Mary" implies a comparison, thereby recognising their separateness. They could be married, and people could say, or they could believe, that they are the same. Sameness only exists in relation to "the other" who, by definition of being "the other", is different—is not "I". For instance, identical twins portray this very clearly: they are identical, but one is not the other, even if parents and those around them dress them alike in order to reinforce sameness.

Parents often say to their offspring: "We treat you exactly the same", "We love you both equally". They are prepared to swear that their love does not harbour favouritism. If we imagine that these parents have two sons, we could further suppose that brother A complains that brother B is mother's favourite. Mother very adamantly reassures both: "Your father and I have never treated you differently, we love you exactly the same! For God's sake stop going on and on about something that is a figment of your imagination." She is prepared to swear to it—this is her conviction. She asks her husband to express his unbiased opinion. He is a good parent and without hesitation agrees with his wife. The situation that I described suggests a view of "very democratic and concerned parents", who have been able to split into equal parts the love and care that they profess for their sons. We can wonder why this is such an important issue for these parents: perhaps this family needs to ensure equal distribution in order to maintain the image of "very good parents" Is it that something very difficult or terrible may occur if differences were to come to the surface? If we think about differences in terms of comparisons, who is going to stop the ill-feelings that these comparisons may generate? Usually there are dreaded conflicts that come to the fore at a conscious or unconscious level.

It is generally accepted among psychoanalysts that the narrative of myths has very important aspects that are useful for the understanding of the unconscious phantasies of individuals in their emotional development. Freud based on the Oedipus myth his ideas about the Oedipus complex, which occupies an important position in psychoanalytic theory and helps to clarify some of the vicissitudes of emotional development, and, in many cases, the way individuals move from the single state to becoming a couple and then how the couple becomes dysfunctional. Sometimes myths convey clearly the ideas that one is trying to explore and describe. I use two well-known myths, which constitute an important aspect of Western culture, to explore the concepts of sameness and difference.

From the point of view of culture and religion, we can consider the story of the creation of the first man and the first woman. God created "Adam in his own image … and God made man from the dust of the earth and blew life through his nostrils, so he became … Adam. He was the first-born", which implies a time-difference with Eve. Following our experiences in child development, we can speculate that God wanted to give Adam a companion and secure human development. The Bible says "it is not good for man to be alone". So God decided to give him a female companion to be with. He took a rib from Adam when he was asleep and from it made Eve. We can wonder what the world would have been like if God had made the woman first and from her rib made the first man. In relation to this, I want to mention an experience I had that shows the difficulties of dealing with similarities and differences, in this case the difference of male and female identity at a socio-cultural and emotional level. I remember that when I was part of a health group that was trying to help the Nicaraguans in their new government, we took a minicab and the driver asked if he could briefly stop in three places before going to our destination. We agreed, and we learned that this driver was looking after three women who were his partners and with whom he had several children. Women's role until that point had been to clean the house, look after the young children, and to stay at home. A year later we learned that the government had encouraged women to come out of their houses, shed their passive attitude, and take a more active role in society. We were surprised that this important change activated a massive increase in alcoholism and psychological breakdown in men. They could not cope with the change; the difference that this change brought to their relationship was overwhelming for the men.

Therefore, in relation to Adam and Eve we can see the similarities and the differences. Following the Bible, Cain and Abel are their sons. Cain works the land and Abel is a shepherd. God accepts the offering made by Abel but does not accept Cain's. Cain kills his brother. Difference is associated with rivalry and rejection. The likelihood is that when parents assert their view that "we love them exactly the same", they are trying to make sure that they are not encouraging feelings of rivalry and rejection.

Similarities and differences at a marital level

All these different manifestations can come into the open at different stages of the life cycle, but they can be noticeable earlier on in life, as was highlighted by Melanie Klein in her work with small children. Quite often they are exacerbated in marital relationships. For instance, some partners cannot tolerate that the other may be better-looking or have better qualities. For instance, Jane comes to mind: she has a full-time job; her husband, who has been made redundant, is looking after their nine-year-old twins. He seems to be doing a good job in terms of being a good father, and Jane is extremely angry about this.

Sometimes individuals choose a partner with serious problems in order to feel superior, or to feel that they can cure or help them. Sometimes they need to have someone who is similar—either to avoid rivalry, or as an easy way to project their own problems or pathologies. The possibilities are numerous. It is important to explore whether the couple had a good relationship in the past, when that good relationship stopped, and why it came to an end.

It is also important to be aware that men and women are likely to develop different symptoms and emotional responses to similar stressful situations or traumas in their marital life or in their respective lives. This is due to the biological and psychological differences between them. Sometimes this can be a source of conflict in their marital interaction.

Psychoanalysis has shown how perceptions of the other are misconstrued by our own projections. When this mechanism is very intense in the marital interaction, it creates a distorted view that hinders the capacity to integrate experiences and perceptions. These experiences and perceptions may be badly negotiated and integrated by the marital partner if the anxieties are too great due to the intensity of the projections or the psychological balance.

In relation to social and cultural issues, it is important to acknowledge that in recent decades we have been witnessing significant structural changes in families and marital couples, brought about by economic, technological, and cultural changes. Patriarchal society has changed—something that is more noticeable in the large cities of the Western world. In the past, men used to be the money-earners and the dominant figures; women were dedicated to looking after the house, their children, and their husbands. In recent decades a significant development has taken place: women have started to go out to work, and this has brought about considerable structural changes that affect individuals, marital and family relationships, and society.

At the same time, it is important to acknowledge that there are communities of different cultures and ethnicities where the individual, marital, and family expectations differ from the culture that exists in the West. Practitioners are required to be aware of these ethnic and cultural variations and the possible sensitive effects on identity, gender, sexuality, and social class. For instance, as mentioned above, McGoldrick (1998) equates the concept of ethnicity with a combination of race, religion, history, myths, language, and more. Some of these aspects come to be interwoven at a conscious and unconscious level and affect individual, marital, and family identities, historical continuity, filiations, and real or fictitious values.

In relation to these issues, it is important to note the growing number of intermarriages arising from massive migrations due to wars and difficult economic situations.

I will give a clinical example that shows the similarities and differences in a couple facing a sense of loss. The two partners came from different cultures, and both sets of parents had migrated from different countries. The wife was the leader and the husband followed her.

Husband: "What were you thinking? Today is the thirtieth of March."
   Wife: "I know. Today is the anniversary of our son's death. I was thinking about it this morning. Today he would have been twenty-three years old. I tried to imagine him at this age."

Husband: "I still find it so difficult and so painful. I remember that I was holding him in my arms when he died. The nurse asked if I wanted to stay in his room: I am a doctor and I said yes. He was dead! I was crying. Looking at him, I was remembering when he was a baby and I never held him in my arms."

Therapist: "This seems the worst thing that has happened in your lives." (Both agree.)

Wife: "Yes, by far!"

Therapist: "Thinking about it, what do you think has been the effect it had on you?"

Wife: "It has brought us closer. It made us to appreciate our children a lot more. Perhaps I was frightened of losing them. That is when we came to you the first time."

Husband: "I resent when they show their independence. Both are exactly the same, only a year and a half apart. They will finish their university careers soon. I do resent that they have already left home and have their independent lives. I would want to have them here at home."

Wife: "I know that they are not the same, they have different personalities! But I still keep their school notes from primary school and still keep some of their clothes from when they were small children. I know it is silly. I cannot give them away."

Therapist: (I commented that some of their losses are very difficult to overcome and, for the husband, their capacity to be independent.) "Your wife is the leader, and is the one who makes the family decisions. Your husband is the follower, and he seems to be pleased that you decide for him and for you. There is no conflict about it."

(Both agreed.)

Therapist: "No conflict between you is very important. No differences. In addition I am wondering if you have made of your lives and your family some sort of mausoleum dedicated to Daniel. You battled and did not want your children to be different or to leave home."

Wife: "Yes! It was a big struggle. I did not want them to leave home; they were not ready and we are not ready."

Therapist: "It seems that the empty nest produced by the children who left home is connected in your minds with the death of your first child, and if you acknowledge their differences, it will bring these differences into the open. The problem seems to be the possible differences between you. Too much anxiety!"

Wife: "I did not think about it in this way, but perhaps yes. There are too many issues, and it feels too much at this stage in our lives."

Therapist: "When I referred to Daniel's death that activated an attitude in you equivalent to a mausoleum it was a bit unfair because after the dead child you managed to produce two children and therefore you took a risk."

(Both husband and wife nodded in agreement and looked at each other.)

Therapist: "But now there is a huge pain because they left home and again you are now a couple, in terms of living together face to face in your house. Are you frightened to bring differences between your children or you as husband and wife that could activate a disaster?"

These two individuals have their own personalities and their own individual and family histories. Therefore, they enter into the couple relationship with their own value system, or, in metaphorical terms, both have brought their own luggage: they have been influenced or affected by their own families of origin, as well as other contexts. I am emphasising the complexity of the possible interactive pressures. The most important positive issue that was the main focus at this stage was their ability to negotiate losses and differences in a constructive way, and the way they could understand and support each other about these issues. I was aware that I was helping to deal with the effect of a traumatic loss. But the man's need to stay in the back row at home and the woman's to be in the front row, the one that made decisions, was an issue that was developed later on in their treatment.

There are different types of couples. From a historical perspective it becomes important to know the couple's social, cultural, religious, and ethnic backgrounds, their individual, family, and social expectations, and how they became a couple. The way they behave towards their families of origin and towards other couples will point to their own identity as a couple. Sometimes we observe an intense need, mixed with eagerness and excitement, towards establishing a couple relationship. We can also observe the opposite reaction, which can take place either before the couple relationship is established or afterwards. It can be quite in the open or be out of sight. What emotions fuel one type of emotional reaction and what emotions fuel the other are very important to explore in terms of individual, marital, and possible family developments.

We can also observe that when two individuals establish an ongoing relationship, there is the possibility of a basic complementary or symmetrical relationship. This can be positive and lead to mutual support and expression of loving and harmonious feelings, or it can be negative and lead to the opposite, in terms of mutual disqualification and hostile interaction. Another possibility is that one member of the couple is overly dependent on the other. His or her interaction may portray an over-involved or even enmeshed way of relating, or the opposite: independent and distant. A partner may complain that the other never listens and is only concerned with his or her own things. Alternatively, one partner may be verbally, physically, or sexually abusive and the other may react in a submissive way; or there may be an ongoing abusive interaction between the two partners. They may be repeating patterns experienced in their families of origin without being aware of it.

The following clinical material highlights an aspect of the differences within the marital relationship:

> "I want to tell you that I bought tickets to go to the theatre next Saturday!" David announced to his wife, Mary.
>
> "Are you trying to make amends because you stopped my parents from coming to our party last night? I know that you are very critical of them. You don't like them! You must be feeling guilty!" Mary retorted with sarcasm.
>
> "No! I don't have any reasons to feel guilty, and therefore I am not making amends—we simply haven't been to the theatre for a long time, and I thought that you might like that I bought tickets to go to the theatre next Saturday!" David bitterly replied.
>
> "What are we going to see?" asked Mary.
>
> David: *"As You Like It."*
>
> Mary: "I knew it! You know I am fed up with seeing Shakespeare, and I don't like comedies. How many times have I said that?" Sarcastically: "I am sure that this is news to your ears. Your formula is me, me, and always me. You don't have any consideration for what I would like. And you do the same things with holidays. When we met, it was quite different. You were so thoughtful, eager to please me, to anticipate my tastes, and fulfil my wishes, and I did the same. We liked the same things. It is so different now.

Now you behave like the brochure that advertised this fantastic holiday and when you arrive everything is so squalid that you feel you have been taken for a ride."

David: "This is your version. Mine is quite different. I was some form of useful convenience, to satisfy your extravagant taste. To tell you the truth, in relation to your taste, I prefer mine, as I prefer my friends to yours. What a fool! At the end of the day I have only myself to blame!"

Mary: "I am fed up with your constant recriminations, your friends, your work, your football. Everything comes first. You are so selfish and cruel! I am so unhappy! I hate you!"

I have just described a marital interaction in a marital session. Such an interaction can be described as a form of crisis—a type of crisis that can take place in some marriages. In the above-mentioned interaction, we are confronted with a conflict that escalates in intensity and comes to an end without resolution. After a period of calm, in the future something will trigger a similar type of interaction. From a therapeutic perspective, we can produce various hypotheses and several therapeutic interventions, depending on the theoretical stance and style of the therapist. In relation to the present subject, we can see that there are significant differences between the partners that they find difficult to negotiate or integrate because they lack an empathic understanding that could lead them to accept their differences. Their intolerance and resentment favours the ongoing tension or crisis between them.

If we consider that similarity refers to what is alike, in the marital context it means that one partner behaves or looks like the other; this could be positive and could lead to a positive construction and both can feel happy about it or, alternatively, it could be flat, repetitive, and monotonous and block the possibility of positive growth. This could make them unhappy or angry. Difference refers to what is not the same, what does not resemble: it refers to variation and can lead to anger and destruction within the marital relationship. Alternatively, it may lead to the opposite: it can be constructive and enrich the marital relationship. When similarity has been achieved through discussion and conflict resolution, there is a constructive experience that opens the door to the couple's healthy functioning. Both similarities and differences underlie our perception and therefore are very important aspects of our human experience.

CHAPTER TWO

External and internal migration in couples

The Bible refers to the first migration, when Adam and Eve were seduced by the serpent into eating from the tree of knowledge. When their eyes were opened, they were able to see that the materials that make up life are good and evil. Their acquired knowledge had a high price: leaving paradise. The meaning of "paradise" is absolute perfection; therefore, everything is provided in terms of goodness and pleasure.

Life confronts us with migration from birth to death. We can consider that the baby inside the womb experiences a different world: the baby's habitat may resemble a paradise, where everything flows without effort. To be born is to enter a new world, where early attachments and frustrations require external and internal help for these to be worked through. Therefore, we can consider that the first migration takes place when the baby is born: coming out of the womb is a form of migration into a different world. Of course, we sometimes long for a "paradise experience", and on some occasions individuals can recreate illusions or delusions in which some form of paradise can be reinstalled.

Bion's concept of "container" (1970, p. 72) is extremely important to understand the function of Winnicott's concepts of the "good-enough mother" (1971, p. 10), which gives the baby "the capacity to be alone".

This means that the mother stops being the baby's ideal object or possession. Mother tries to understand and help her baby to cope and deal with the loss of the ideal object or paradise. The baby will experience frustration in relation to feeding or, later on, when he or she discovers that mother has a partner. But being a wife does not stop her being a good mother. Melanie Klein described how important are the processes of projections and introjections, which arouse anxiety due to the various potential frustrations: the loss, first, of the breast, when it is not available and is not the baby's total possession; then the mother; and, later, both parents. Mother's empathic capacity and, later on, the empathic capacity of both parents make an extremely important contribution to a healthy development. In other words, this is an important step in psychological growth. All this implies some form of internal migration and will affect migrations further on in life.

We define migration in everyday language as a forced or voluntary move whereby an individual or a family change their habitat. Usually, the previous home and the new one are inextricably intertwined in the mind of the migrant. The state of those left behind, the way the migrant leaves, the way he is viewed by those left behind, how he lands, and the way he is received are going to affect the migrant and the development of the migration. Migration is affected by a number of possible pressures at an individual, family, social, and cultural level and, on the negative side, can raise prejudices, misunderstandings, and considerable conflict. Migration can also produce an enriching experience in terms of helping development and activating a creative perspective.

How the individual and significant others deal with all these possible developments will depend on their inner resources and capabilities. Therefore, this poses the question of how organised or disorganised the individual was before the migration took place: was this a forced migration, a voluntary one, a positive move, a search for new developments, an omnipotent change, a running away? Needless to say, this is going to activate conscious and unconscious wishes and phantasies that, in connection with his resources and capabilities, are going to play a significant role in how the individual is going to organise or reorganise his life in the new habitat and determine whether or not it will become a situation of exile.

As I have mentioned, I consider migration from a dual point of view: the external change of habitat, which activates a psychological or internal change of habitat. The mental change is related to the vicissitudes that the external change brings about; the concept of internal migration refers to the emotional vicissitudes associated with changes, which mean losses or gains. Internal migration can also be linked to different aspects of the Oedipus complex, and in considering a successful internal migration we are also referring to the ability to work though the anxieties aroused by the Oedipus complex.

Locating internal migration at various stages of the life cycle is very important because psychological needs, expectations, and conscious and unconscious fears will vary at different points through life, as the child becomes an adolescent and then an adult who, in time, is confronted with middle and then older age. Understanding this is very important if we want to know how these needs, expectations, and fears will affect the individual's capacity to deal with the various stages. From this perspective, the early years and early development, in terms of attachment and separation and how this is worked through, are especially important in relation to future developmental stages and conflicts. I use an object relations approach developed by Melanie Klein and her followers, but I also stress the importance of different contributions from a psychodynamic and systemic perspective.

Following the object relations approach we know that the first object is the breast and then the mother and the baby is the object; this brings about a dialectic interaction in which each affects the other. This interaction is internalised and becomes part of the intra-psychic or internal world, as well as being projected into the outside world. Therefore, we can say that the couple is the first relation of the human being, and the early emotional development of each partner is going to affect future emotional developments and, along these lines, is going to play a significant role in the couple's interaction.

According to Pichon-Rivière (1961, 1970), this duality brings forward the presence of "the third" that threatens the relationship, or the ratio, of two (meaning the parental couple). In his lectures Pichon-Rivière often stressed that "noise" is always present in any communication; it can manifest as noise, ghost, or fantasy, consciously or unconsciously. Therefore, the basic structure of an individual's development is a dyadic relationship that contains in its structure the notion of "the third". The concept of the third has been acknowledged by several authors; Britton's contribution, in this area, among others, is very important. How individuals deal with the emotional expression of what comes from within and what comes from outside plays a major role in their future development. Within this perspective, working through the Oedipus complex is an essential developmental task that fosters the capacity to grow and the ability to face and deal with anxieties brought about by loss and the arrival of new situations. Normality and pathology unravel through the complexities of the Oedipus complex.

This brings to mind the following clinical example:

> A patient referred to our local clinic was a young woman who had been born in India and had come to the UK when she was a small child. From her description, I formed the view that her family had reinforced their religious beliefs and their original culture when they migrated to the UK. She was the eldest of several siblings and described an oppressive situation at home: her mother criticised her non-stop and demanded so many things from her that she felt she could never satisfy her. There were constant arguments, and her mother tried to stop her from going out and socialising. Her father seemed at first to have taken an outsider's attitude, but when the family learned that the girl had started a relationship with an English boy whom she had met at university, the father and the mother joined forces. Soon after this, she left home and moved to a girlfriend's flat; a month later she and her boyfriend moved in together. At this point, her family cut off all contact with her.
>
> An interesting development was that there was a gradual change of attitude in the girl towards her partner as she increasingly identified with her mother's attitudes and views. She became very argumentative and demanding, and nothing he did satisfied her. Quite significantly, she started to assert her parents' culture in terms of food and social relations.
>
> After several months her attitude and views were so radical that the situation between her and her boyfriend became unmanageable, and their relationship broke up. At first she returned to live with her parents, and after few months she left home and went to live with a female friend.

In this example we can consider the possible emotional disturbances in the patient, and in the mother and the father, related to their psychic structures. At the same time, what seems noticeable are the disturbances possibly caused by the parents' cultural and family background, related to their attachment to their home country and to the difficulties of settling in and making a good attachment to their new habitat. There are also issues associated to their ethnicity and religion. When a family migrates, children tend to find the process of adaptation to the new environment easier than do the parents. They learn the new language more quickly, and they also feel at home in the new environment. However, they can lose touch with, or disengage from, what they have left behind.

Another clinical example along the same lines relates to a consultation I did regarding another young woman who was in psychotherapy with a colleague.

> The patient was born in the UK. Her parents had come from India, and they had settled in the UK many years ago. She became a university professor and when she started a relationship with an Englishman, her family could not bear her "lack of respect". While she did not go along with her family's attitude and was clear about her own views, she felt very distressed about her family's reaction. She was very close to her family, and prior to this situation she had had a good relationship with both her parents. It was clear that there were good bonds between her and her family. The patient went to live with her boyfriend; subsequently they were married and had children. She tried to get help for the entire family, but they refused. At a more distant level, their relationship continued.

This case shows a different attitude from the previous one. This patient was aware of the family's external and internal conflicts, and she was more at home or content with her own views and development. The first case suggests problems of migration in the family and in the patient. The patient was trying to adjust to her Western life, but the cross-cultural experience was not accepted by her family, and there were obvious emotional problems, on the part both of the parents and of their daughter, exacerbated by the migration to a different culture. In the second case, I formed the impression that the parents' migration was not easy: emotionally they struggled to deal with it and with their daughter's independence. But they felt less disturbed than did the parents in the first case, and the daughter was better equipped to deal with the emotional conflict with her parents.

León and Rebeca Grinberg (1989) stressed the importance of developing a good relation to internal objects that facilitates the capacity to deal with losses and acceptance of the new situation. They linked this to the process of migration that requires the capacity to integrate the new country and to accept the loss of what has been left behind. In the second case, the mother felt less troubled than her husband, probably because she continued in her role as a mother, and therefore her sense of identity was less disrupted in comparison with that of her husband. Adult and elderly men often find it difficult to develop a new and suitable role in a new country.

The Oedipus complex draws our attention to many different aspects of human emotions that activate different types of behaviour, ranging from love, hate, rivalry, jealousy, blindness, deceit, lies, "turning a blind eye" (Steiner, 1993), migration, and exile to opening one's eyes and facing reality. The Oedipus myth relates to the process of becoming a couple, a family, filicide, adoption, parricide, and incest. Working through the Oedipus complex, following Melanie Klein's contribution, is the capacity to work through the paranoid-schizoid to the depressive position, which means, in a nutshell, the recognition of opposing feelings and phantasies of love and hate and separateness from the object.

More recently, Fonagy and Target (2003) have developed the concept of mentalisation, which refers to the recognition of one's own emotions and the emotions of significant others. Anxieties appear and reappear throughout the life cycle, and are significant in relation to the present subject of internal and external migration.

I would also like to mention two important contributions: Bion's (1963, 1970) concept of "container and contained" and Ron Britton's (1989, 1998, 2003) concept of the "third position". Bion's notion of "container–contained", as the result of projective identification and introjective identification, is a two-body relationship. If there is a good relationship between container and contained, then this gives rise to a third object. If the relationship between the container and contained and this third object is good, it works to the benefit of all three of them. It requires the empathic capacity of the object, first the mother and then the father, to introduce the position of the subject without abandoning their roles. This model is used in psychotherapy and psychoanalysis, and it refers to the capacity to contain patients' projections and empathically connect with the patient to understand how she or he is feeling without abandoning the professional role. The experience of transference and counter-transference is very important, because the analyst or psychotherapist can explore what is happening and be aware if there is a projective identification or a manipulation to seduce or trap him or her. But if this capacity fails or is not available, then projections can become very destructive: the containing object may fail to accept the projections or may devour, enslave, or annihilate the coping capacities of the subject. These situations are often common in analysis where the patient's phantasy is of being at the mercy of the analyst; at the same time, we also see this type of interaction in couples when one partner experiences the other in a similar way.

Britton's contribution (2003) is his reference to the third position in the oedipal situation. This third position gives the capacity to see and to empathise and the possibility of objectivity and flexibility.

Another significant concept linked to internal migration is narcissism. There is a great deal of divergence in relation to the understanding of narcissism. Britton (2003) made a significant contribution to the third position and differentiated narcissistic personality disorder from borderline disorder and schizoid disorder. He also acknowledged H. Rosenfeld's (1965) distinction between libidinal narcissism and pathological or very destructive narcissism. He focussed on the early object relations and the fact that when the sense of containment is deeply affected, the likelihood is that the narcissistic libidinal development is going to be affected, and the individual is going to develop a destructive narcissistic organisation. I consider that the individual developing this destructive narcissistic organisation is going to disrupt or block the possibilities of external and internal migrations.

Throughout the various different types of migrations, it is important for the individual to be able to maintain his sense of identity and this requires a degree of healthy narcissism. At the same time, there needs to be a capacity to grow and to integrate all the various external and internal changes that can affect the sense of identity in a positive way.

Developing a couple relationship or getting married are, metaphorically, forms of migration, in terms of the expectations and pressures that affect both members. For both partners, getting married means a change of external and internal habitat; at a conscious and unconscious level it is often a complex phenomenon that can also affect and be affected by both partners' significant relationships. Marriage is a social relationship that includes two partners, with their own personalities and their own individual and family histories. In addition, other contexts—ethnic, racial, social, religious, cultural, and historical—can also contribute, directly or indirectly, to their interaction. Every couple has its own identity—an identity linked to both partners' individual interactions and emotional developments and the effect that external pressures have on them.

The exploration of each partner's conscious and unconscious fantasies about becoming a couple provides a view of their individual identities and mental interactions within the couple relationship. Their projective and introjective identifications play a significant part in their capacity for intimacy, for tolerating separateness, and for their mutuality in terms of their creative or destructive interactions. Quite often, people experience a wish, desire, or need to establish a close, stable, intimate relationship with another person with whom they would like to share aspects of their lives, have new experiences, and construct a future life. This brings up the question: What brought these two people to migrate and form a couple relationship or to separate? This brings with it other relevant questions, such as: When?, Why?, What for? Possible answers to these questions are likely to involve relevant gains or losses.

Some of the familiar questions that we may come across are:

- Is this a new development of a loving experience?
- Is this a way of coping with a previous rejection?
- Is this a covenant marriage, civil or religious?
- Is this an alliance for economic convenience or social achievement?
- Is this a desperate link to guard against loneliness?
- Is this a way of leaving home?
- Is this a coming together because the couple need to migrate?
- Is this a way of coping with unresolved trauma?
- Is this a search for narcissistic gratification?
- Is this a way to revive past issues?
- Is this a way to find in the other a depository of unwanted or intolerable aspects?
- Is this a way of recreating bad experiences, such as physical or sexual abuse?
- Is this a loving interaction and development and therefore a way to create and recreate new experiences?
- Is this a way to create a family?
- Is this a way of getting at one or the other partner's parents?
- Is this a way of finding a convenient hook for problems?

From a systemic perspective we can say that marriage is a subsystem of the family as well as a system in its own right. The way a couple's views, emotions, behaviours, communications, and miscommunications affect and organise their patterns of interaction adds further understanding to the marital relationship and its problems. When we look at a subsystem, it is important to explore its relations to other subsystems and to the system as a whole.

The couple's respective roles and role interaction are also important. A role is a behavioural unit that emerges through a mixture of cultural, social, and family expectations, in interaction with the individual's experience and perceptions. There are open or explicit aspects to all this, and there are also unconscious and hidden areas that have a significant effect. When observing the partners' interactions, it is important to explore their respective roles and how their views of the role of husband and wife compare with how they view the roles of their own fathers and mothers, grandfathers and grandmothers. Another aspect to be explored is how migration from one role to another has been worked through, and how the couple's roles have been affected by this migration. But migration is a complex phenomenon, and I focus only on certain aspects that I think are significant within the therapeutic field.

First of all, I want to clarify that migration and change are not the same. Migration is a more complicated phenomenon and refers to different aspects of change. External migration is a change of a geographical habitat and refers to a series of different, complicated possibilities that will affect the outcome. Internal migration refers to a series of emotional reactions at a conscious and unconscious level that will be mobilised and will affect the outcome.

Migration has been studied from various angles—sociological, anthropological, economic, cultural, religious, and so on. It has also been studied from a psychological or psychoanalytic perspective. I find the book by Léon and Rebeca Grinberg, *Psychoanalytic Perspectives on Migration and Exile* (1989), very helpful. The authors describe the internal process of migration and the interaction with external process and pressures. In this book, I have followed their lines of exploration.

I am also informed by my psychoanalytic understanding of different types of migration where the main focus is on the psychic vicissitudes of dealing with various forms of migration and by my experience in the NHS with families, couples, and individuals who had elected to migrate and those who had been forced to migrate. I am also informed by my own personal experience in terms of internal and external migration.

When my parents migrated to a new country, met there, and were married, the prevailing view was that social, cultural, and religious similarities provided a natural context for marital compatibility. At that time, unless war or other circumstances forced people to make a geographical migration, partners tended to share the same social background, religion, and cultural values and live in a similar habitat. This socio-cultural attitude was reinforced by literature and romantic films that conveyed the view that the romantic marriage promised some form of paradise: "You are my soul" ... "You are my life."

In more recent decades, great technological developments in many areas, including the media and the globalised economy, have created a form of globalised culture. Among the many significant socio-cultural changes throughout the world, an important one is migration, which has resulted in an increased number of mixed marriages from different ethnicities, religions, races, cultures, and, to some extent, social classes. These changes have been the source of different types of conflicts both within marriage and outside, but it is important to acknowledge that when these conflicts are overcome, they can offer the possibility of enriched and creative relationships.

The traditional view that you marry forever has also changed—so much so that a sign of our times is that almost half of marriages end in divorce, and most parents spend less time with their children. In recent decades we have been witnessing massive geographical migrations due to wars and economic situations. Nuclear families are getting smaller; extended families exist only in underdeveloped countries or small villages. Other important changes are the acceptance of gay partnerships and the legalisation of gay marriages in some countries, and the role of women in industrialised countries. Nowadays most women are employed and work as hard as men, pursue fulfilling careers, and, in some cases, may be the main breadwinner of the family. In many couple relationships, this can be a source of conflict.

As mentioned at the beginning of this chapter, the Bible makes important references to migration: for instance, Adam and Eve are seduced into eating from the tree of knowledge. When their eyes are opened, they are able to see that the materials that make up life are good and evil. This newly acquired knowledge costs them dearly: the price is leaving paradise, the characteristics of which were absolute goodness and total pleasure. We sometimes long for paradise, and individuals and couples can recreate illusions or delusions in which some form of paradise (as they see it) can be reinstalled.

Migration has been a part of the life of humankind since its origins. When people stopped being nomads and settled down in one territory and then later moved to another place, this was the beginning of actual geographical migration.

Every important move is likely to activate a complex process where internal anxieties about losses, and anxieties about what is to come or is new, are going to interact with the external situation. This could be welcoming or rejecting in a broad sense.

When we say "to settle down and feel at home", we are implying that the person feels comfortable with his or her own self. We can say that this is the aim of every individual. The possibility of being yourself in terms of identity, and feeling at home with yourself in your new situation or your new habitat, is the aim of a successful migration.

As we have seen, migration is a forced or a voluntary move whereby the individual changes his or her habitat. Any type of migration activates anxiety, the level of which varies according to many different external and internal circumstances: in many cases anxieties can escalate and lead to intense emotional outbursts and derailments at the individual, marital, family, and society levels.

In relation to "external migration", it is important to take into account the state of those left behind, how each partner or the couple leave their previous habitat, how they land in their new place, and how they are received. In relation to "internal migration", it is significant how the individual is going to deal with all these possible developments in terms of his or her inner resources and capabilities:

- How emotionally organised or disorganised was the individual before the migration took place?
- Was the individual persecuted, or was her or his psychic pain too difficult to tolerate?
- Did developmental pressure to change feel too much in the family contexts?

The two basic questions are: How is the individual going to deal with anxieties aroused by what the individual or family left behind—that is, deal with losses? How is she or he going to deal with what is new or different in the new habitat—that is, with change? Sometimes there are idealised or manic views that colour the new habitat or new experience.

We often see people who try to re-establish what they have left behind; they avoid anything that is new, because it is new or because they feel overwhelmed by it. Then we also often see the opposite reaction: everything has to be different. The possibilities are many, depending on the external and internal circumstances.

Exile in traditional terms means a forced migration, a lack of freedom. "Internal exile" refers to the inability of the individual's internal resources to deal with the pressures, anxieties, and uncertainties aroused by migration.

Two case studies can serve as examples.

Mr A: Clinical example

Patient: I have been thinking during the weekend about the last session: the reference to Hitler and various types of dictatorships: Idi Amin, Saddam Hussein in Iraq and the present one in Iran. You were right, I need power and I love power. Otherwise, I lack confidence in myself. I know that money is very important to me, and I manage to make money in very difficult times. My business has done well. My wife loves material things; I buy expensive things for the house and the cottage and especially for her, and we go to exotic places that she likes to go to. I shut her mouth in this way, and she has to follow me. I know that this is my way of controlling her, and I have the power to do so. In this way I feel that I can do my things and not be imprisoned by her. I am British, and she comes from an undeveloped country. I know that this is not right.

Mr A continued talking and bringing forward issues we have seen several times in previous sessions. I suggested that in the way he had been talking, it gave me the impression that he was telling me what he had imagined I would like to hear; then I would make some analytic interpretations that he would automatically acknowledge and create an impression in me and him of an apparently very good psychoanalytic interaction. In this way, he manages to be in control and in power, and he ensures that my interpretations are not going to touch him. He acknowledged what I suggested, but it felt flat. Nevertheless I did notice his quick gesture and a sudden tension in his body. I drew his attention to what had happened, and he went along with what I suggested, but the tension in his body did not go along with it. He made a sound of acknowledgment. I suggested that once again he tried to seduce me with what he imagined I would like to hear in order to be in control and have power, perhaps like some sort of tyrant. Otherwise, he fears that he will be imprisoned by me, just as he fears that if he did not seduce and conquer his wife with expensive presents that she likes or airline tickets to her own country, he will be imprisoned by her. He agreed.

At one level there is a couple-relationship between patient and analyst. Then there is a reference to his marital relationship.

In relation to Mr A's family of origin, his father was a diplomat, and therefore the family was often on the move and the children were looked after by childminders. Apparently the father was strict and peripheral, and he died when Mr A was an adolescent. He was the youngest of three siblings and could only escape from his mother's powerful attachment to him by continuing his studies in another city. The school provided some form of migration and containment but kept his parents and family at a distance. There is a clear identification with his father, who kept his wife under control, as he did with his mother. Towards his wife and his children he has the same attitude as his father had. The reason for seeking help was an illness that connected him to his father.

I imagine that Mr A's sense of home was built up by a sense of an omnipotent kingdom, through his ability to earn money. Apparently he was very good at making sculptures, but this did not provide him with money. He identified with his father and tried to copy his eldest sister, who made more money than he, but he kept her at a distance to avoid rivalry with her. My impression is that the lack of containment and support in his early relationships contributed to Mr A's vulnerability and lack of confidence in relationships.

If we consider that settling in a new environment, getting married, and developing a family represent a form of migration, we see the emotional struggles and coping mechanisms that suggest that Mr A's migrations were not entirely successful.

From a psychological perspective, entering into a couple relationship and marriage is a form of migration. Some individuals use the couple as a bridge to have a family. Along these lines, for a woman to have her first baby or to create a family is also a form of migration. Becoming a couple mobilises anxieties at many different levels and requires adjustments to a new mental state. Looking at migration from the individual psycho-developmental perspective—as in the example of Mr A—enables us to understand some of the vicissitudes that occur when people get married. Sometimes the marriage and the new family is their attempt to develop and grow, but their efforts show the difficulties of establishing a successful migration.

Mrs. N. and Mr. B

Mrs. N and Mr. B were a married couple in their late forties. They had migrated from Spain, and they had three adolescent children who were born in the UK. They requested help regarding their son Peter. They said that this was the only problem that was affecting them. I saw the whole family first, and then I saw the parents without their children.

I bring material from one of their sessions. Peter was still in the adolescent unit as an inpatient; he was fifteen, and he had become very manic in a disco. Apparently he and other youngsters had been drinking heavily, and it was not clear whether they were under the influence of drugs; the police had to intervene. The couple described how shocked they were with everything that had happened and talked about Peter's disturbed behaviour and his ongoing emotional problems. He had been a source of worry since he was a child.

I acknowledged the very worrying and difficult situation that they endured as parents and their need for help. I tried to explore this situation from different angles, but they continued talking about it in an intense and emotionally animated way. I suggested that perhaps without knowing it, individually and as a couple, they were using Peter's problems in order not to attend to issues of their own as a couple.

They were baffled by what I suggested; they looked at each other and did not agree. Mrs. N said that Peter's main problem was his lack of boundaries. I reminded them that we had discussed in the previous session the lack of clear boundaries between them, and it became clear that this issue was present from the beginning of their marital relationship. Mrs. N said that maybe I was right. ... When they had moved to the UK, everything had changed between them. It felt as if the good times belonged to their early history in Barcelona. Mr. B had become distant and authoritarian. However, since they had been coming to therapy, she felt that they have been working at these issues, and there was an improvement in these areas. In relation to Thomas and Lola, the other two children, they were doing better in their studies, learning English better and more quickly, and the relationship between them had improved. Thomas and his father were also getting on better. Father agreed and added, "I took him to see a football match, to see the team he supports, which is not the one I support."

I asked them about their couple relationship. Mrs. N said that it had improved. Mr. B nodded in agreement. She said that they had gone together to see Peter at the hospital—this was a new attitude. Before going there, they had done the shopping for the house together—that was also a change.

Then I asked Mr. B about their couple relationship, and he started to talk about Peter and Lola. I made a comment about how difficult the couple relationship was for him, so much so that he used the children to keep it at a distance. I suggested that he had escaped from the couple's interaction by hiding behind his paternal role. Mr. B is the older of two siblings. His sister had suffered from asthma as a child, and the parents were over-involved with her. On several occasions she had to be hospitalised. There was domestic violence at home: the father was violent and physically abused his wife.

"My sister tried to protect our mother in the fights. I shut the door and tried to escape or ignore what was going on, and it was very difficult. I do not have any positive or warm feelings towards my upbringing or my family. When I was thirteen, my parents split up. I enjoyed being at school, and it was good to get into university and interact with other students."

It was clear that the educational institutions had provided Mr. B with a sense of security or safety that he did not have at home. Studying also gave him a sense of self-esteem and fed his narcissistic needs. He also mentioned that he developed a thick skin to protect himself when he was at home.

Mrs. N came from a large family, and she is also the oldest of four siblings. Her mother was a strong woman; her father was always work-ing on the land. She grew up in a small village in Spain. She managed to leave her family at the age of sixteen, went to live with a maternal aunt in Barcelona, and soon after that started to work. She and Mr. B were married while he was still an undergraduate student. When he qualified, she was already pregnant; they migrated to the UK, where he continued with further studies.

Mrs. N said that her parents had had a very good marriage, and there was always a good atmosphere at home, even if her two sisters sometimes quarrelled with each other; she never saw any arguments between her parents. She was taken totally by surprise when, a few years ago, at a family gathering, her two sisters said that she was their father's favourite, the apple of his eye. When she disputed this, they laughed at her. I suggested that at one level she was a good daughter who identified with her parents' strong beliefs and culture; she saw what was going on in the way her parents wanted to her to see it. "My parents often said, 'We are exactly the same with all our children, we do not make any difference and this is a perfect marriage'". She smiled. I suggested that she had camouflaged her rivalry with her mother by identifying with her and becoming just as she described her. She showed the similar style and attitudes.

To develop clear boundaries within the couple and between the couple and the children was the first therapeutic step. There was a particular issue in relation to the danger of Mr. B getting angry, becoming verbally abusive, and losing control—something that had already happened. This was an issue that we discussed, and we both felt confident that it was under control. Another step was to explore the changes they needed the other to make in order to get closer to each other in a safer way and therefore to achieve a safe and constructive migration.

Marriage has been an important step for them—the first important step of migration from their families—and London offered the possibility of creating a new habitat for them.

We discussed their unspoken fantasies of what they expected in this new place and how they imagined their situation would be if they were in their country of origin. I also brought to their attention the interaction of their parents, using role play. I was surprised how determined they were to make this migration work. Their sense of intimacy and expression of love became clearer and improved.

Conclusion

In the marital situation it is very important to explore the partners' individual life cycles and their respective parents' expectations of them as well as their marital and family interactions. I consider the phenomenon of migration from a dual perspective, the external situation and the internal situation. In relation to the external situation, we are aware that migration has opened up the possibility of increasing our understanding of the complexities that a change of habitat or a significant developmental step can bring about, whether at the level of a geographical change, an intermarriage, marriage, or couple relationship. In relation to the internal situation, we are aware that any form of migration activates all sorts of fantasies and anxieties, positive and negative, at a conscious and an unconscious level. At one level there is an important question about the place or situation that was left behind; at another, there is the process of adaptation to a new situation. I have highlighted some of the main areas of stress and the vicissitudes that can affect the different circumstances and different types of individuals.

As I have already mentioned, I consider the concept of migration useful for trying to understand and deal with the external and internal emotional vicissitudes triggered by the concrete experience of a geographical change of habitat and by the changes related to emotional development. I have also stressed the importance of the life cycle, as an important context within which to understand and explore these vicissitudes, which are especially activated in the process of getting married. It is important to underline that the process of migration and its vicissitudes will activate fantasies, which may acquire different meanings according to the stage of the life cycle in which migration is taking place.

CHAPTER THREE

Creativity or the absence of creativity in marital relationships

C reativity is a significant expression of human development and, as such, is determined and influenced by emotional, cultural, and social aspects. Creativity can manifest itself in the individual, the couple, the family, institutions, and the social group and is usually supported or validated by the existing social culture. Creativity refers to the capacity to change or break away from a previous state and find a new solution or a new original view. Creative imagination and the practicalities that allow it to come to fruition connect or come together. When a problem is solved in an original or new way, we are confronted with a creative behaviour. Like many different types of behaviour, creativity is affected and influenced by various aspects of social and cultural systems, in different areas; therefore, the acknowledgment of creativity varies. Creative behaviour indicates that things can be seen, dealt with, or experienced in different ways. The archetype of individual creativity can be seen in Archimedes: born in 287BC, in Syracuse, Archimedes was a Greek mathematician, physicist, engineer, inventor, and astronomer. Although few details of his life are known, he is regarded as one of the leading scientists of classical antiquity. Archimedes was asked to determine whether the king's crown was pure gold or silver with a gold coating. He was having a bath, and he noticed that the level of water was rising as he stepped into the bathtub. From this he deduced that gold and other metals had different densities, and thus he could establish whether the crown was pure gold. He came out of the bath shouting "Eureka!"—meaning: I've got it! I was able to find out!

Creativity typifies a type of behaviour that produces a rupture or a change. This means that in creativity there is a break in the previous state and the possible introduction of a different perspective, which leads, in an original way, to a solution to a problem or to a different viewpoint; in other words, a new road comes to be illuminated. Spontaneity and courage are two contributory aspects of creativity, but they are not the only ones. The acknowledgment of creativity varies, and it can be manifested by different features in a variety of fields: in science, teaching, industry, commerce, art, music, literature, philosophy, psychotherapy, and so on.

The psychoanalytic perspective is an important field in which to explore this issue. In relation to this approach, our focus is creativity or lack of creativity within the couple relationship, and how both partners manage or fail to manage to work through their Oedipus complex. All this is likely to affect their marital relationship and their creative possibilities.

In this context it is important to explore several issues. First, from the beginning of life the individual is not alone, and thus any form of communication expresses a relationship with the other. This implies that the other person or object is going to reply or communicate as some form of response. Therefore, there is a bond or a connection between the two, and thus there is a communication or a relationship that goes in both directions, and both are affected. From a developmental perspective, the baby is affected, the mother is affected, and both affect each other. It is like a spiral that carries on developing from birth onwards. This refers to the mutual capacity of mother and baby to tolerate separateness and value what they receive and what they give to each other. This, then, enables the baby to tolerate the parents' relationship as a parental couple. This has been elaborated by various authors, such as Britton (1989) in terms of the third or the triangular relationship. Second, I want to emphasise the importance of using the life-cycle perspective in terms of chronological phases from infancy onwards in order to explore the individual's emotional development. This development, which is also influenced by individuals' families, friends, and social-cultural factors, has an effect on the capacity to develop a marital relationship and the possibilities of becoming creative.

The creativity of a small child, a ten-year-old child, an adolescent, an adult, a middle-aged or an older person will not be the same. As I have mentioned, from birth onwards individuals are expected to develop in their ability to deal with emotional and biological changes and with external needs and pressures. This emotional development is influenced by the way each partner has negotiated the Oedipus complex, and, directly or indirectly, this can enhance or undermine the creative possibilities of the couple.

I think that narcissism it is quite relevant to our main subject. In relation to narcissism Melanie Klein disagreed with Freud who considered that there was a primary narcissism in infancy before there was recognition of an object. Her view was that the baby's early development is supported by object relations. This manifests in the baby's capacity to work through the relationship with the mother and because this capacity is not absolute it will contribute to the development of libidinal narcissism. Therefore, narcissism is a defence mechanism against dependency. The baby avoids the conflict of dependency, and love is developed towards the self. Healthy narcissism is based on healthy self-love because from this situation the infant is able to develop a healthy object-love which includes the capacity to work through mourning of his or her ideal object. When this situation cannot be transformed in a positive way due to destructive emotions and phantasies, pathological narcissism develops, which activates disturbing emotions, such as persecutory and paranoid anxieties. We can say that both types of narcissisms—libidinal and pathological—fulfil a defensive function against dependency, but there is a significant difference between them. They affect the individual's emotional development and the capacity to work through the oedipal anxieties. As you can imagine, all this is going to play a significant role within the marital vicissitudes and the couple's capacity to become creative.

The classical view, following Klein's and Segal's contributions, highlights the depressive position as the important developmental step that helps the individual to work through ambivalence. In relation to it, hate can be mitigated by love, and therefore losses can be worked through, reparation takes place, and life has a positive outlook. This lends the individual the courage necessary to cope with uncertainty and therefore the possibility to search for and create a new positive outlook.

As Hannah Segal (Segal, 1952, p. 196) wrote: "M. Klein's work, especially her concept of the depressive position, the reparative drives that are set in motion by it, and her description of the world of inner objects, throws new light on the psychology of the artist, on the conditions necessary for him to be successful, and on those which can inhibit or vitiate his artistic activities."

There are varying views about creativity. As Janine Chasseguet-Smirgel (1985) describes it, perversion is associated with false creativity, but she also points out that many perverts are able to produce genuine creations. She suggests that there are some perverts who have a large amount of libido that can be sublimated and used in a creative process. Other types of perverts use their ego ideal as an anal phallus in their creation. In other words, where a normal child or partner would have been able to deal with his or her Oedipus complex, the pervert is able to represent in his or her creations an anal phallus that is above or superior to his or her Oedipal objects. I think that this view is linked to the number of individuals who have not reached their depressive position. Some have developed a pathological character. Couples sometimes present similar characteristics. I have seen occasions where individuals have needed to use or abuse alcohol or take drugs before being able to start a creative activity. Sometimes creative artists present pathological disturbances, but these disturbances do not block their creative capacities. However, the depressive position is a very important developmental state that facilitates the creative possibilities of some individuals, but we should not take a moralistic view in relation to it. Now focusing on the couple, we can see examples where the couple has inspired artists, such as writers, poets, and painters, to give expression to their artistic talents.

In general, we understand that a couple or marital relationship refers to two individuals who develop a special attraction towards each other and decide to live together, to share intimacy, and develop plans for the future; in some cases this includes developing a family. The reference to a marital couple could be defined in a simple and classical way as two people of the opposite sex, but we know that the notion is much more complex than this: there are all sorts of married and unmarried couples.

A psychodynamic understanding plays a significant role in exploring and understanding the conscious and unconscious motivations that lead individuals to develop a couple or marital relationship, as well as their interactions, which can activate a creative activity or a destructive interaction.

In the 1960s, Henry Dicks at the Tavistock Clinic managed to develop a significant psychodynamic approach to marital therapy. This has had a significant influence throughout the world. In Argentina, Puget and Berenstein (1988) contributed further to this subject; they described marital mental functioning within three spaces: (1) "intra-subjective"—referring to object relations, (2) "inter-subjective"—referring to the relationship or bond between different egos, and (3) "trans-subjective"—referring to the bond established within the macro-social and cultural context. These three spaces are very significant within individual emotional development, but they are also very active within the marital relationship.

Marriage and families are important organisations of human structure and when they develop significant disturbances require sensitive and specialised therapists to attend to them. It is important to acknowledge that there are significant differences between the psychoanalytic approach and other approaches, such as systemic or structural, or psychodrama—each with its own theoretical and technical variations—whilst underlining that each of these approaches seeks to develop a better way of dealing with marital difficulties. This might mean getting on better within the therapeutic relationship and improving the couple relationship, thereby allowing creativity to emerge in the relationship, although sometimes a good outcome may lead to separation. It is important for the therapist to be aware that separation could be the expression of a destructive interaction, but it could also, in some cases, be a constructive one. The important issue for the marital therapist is to maintain a neutral attitude and help both members of the couple to work through a sense of loss in order to establish a new constructive interaction.

Sophocles used the Oedipus myth to write his famous plays, *Oedipus Rex* and *Oedipus at Colonus*. When Sophocles was very old, not long before he died, it is possible that his creativity was in tune with issues that were affecting him at that stage of his life, manifesting as significant themes in the plays. Sophocles' plays, and the various understandings of the Oedipus myth, convey different views and versions that highlight various possibilities of understanding individual emotional development as it is created by external facts and unconscious fantasies.

The first struggle in life is for the newborn baby to recognise a separate object. Each individual's life starts as a couple: mother and baby. At this stage the outsider is the father; but eventually the baby is confronted with the view that both parents are together, and the baby is helped by them to recognise that husband and wife are also the parents and to cope with that experience. Klein, Winnicott, Bion, and, more recently, Britton, among others, made significant references to this type of experience from the point of view of object relations and the significance of the third. In addition, they consider that working through the Oedipus complex also meant reaching the depressive position. It is important to underline that this is an ongoing process.

Bion also made an important contribution in the area of knowledge, which he designates with the letter "K." In relation to the triangular space described by Britton, Ruszczynski (2005) has suggested that this space can be adapted to the couple when they are able to develop an intimate relationship. He called it "the marital triangle". This refers to the partners as two individuals and their relationship as the third element. "The *capacity* to achieve this state, to create the space within the marital triangle and to be able to be a creative couple, if achievable, could be said to be developmental stage in its own right" (Ruszczynski, 2005, p. 42, original emphasis).

Once again, I want to make a reference to Bion's contribution. He drew attention to the importance of the joined need of therapist and patient to be surprised and to be encouraged to have an appetite to learn more. When this takes place, we are in the land of therapeutic creativity. It is also important to acknowledge that in certain situations the possibility of learning from previous knowledge can have a negative effect and block the therapeutic possibilities. Ruszczynski (2005) made a reference to Kernberg's (1993) description of a couple in its own right, and along these lines the couple acquires its identity. He also mentioned that Kernberg described a healthier, more positive couple relationship, which implies an internalisation of a good object relation based on internal connections with their original couple—the parents—and also refers to disturbances that come to the fore when the good experience is lacking.

Metaphorically, both members of a couple bring to the marital relationship their own baggage of conscious and unconscious experiences. M. Morgan (2005) stresses the importance of symmetry in terms of both partners being able to acknowledge and to cope in a positive way with their similarities and differences. It is also important to pay attention to the obvious steps within the life cycle. It is very different if the couple relationship has developed in very young adulthood, in adulthood, in middle age or older age, and if they have been together for only a year, or for five, twenty, or forty years. The likelihood is that each partner has gone through adolescence before she or he settles into a stable couple relationship. Adolescence is a very important stage of development due to the significant pressures and changes at the psychological, biological, family, and socio-cultural levels. For this reason, I consider that the process of development of the adolescent requires considerable adjustment, and many marital problems can be traced to this particular stage.

In relation to the psychological changes that take place in adolescence, an important one is development of the individual's own identity. This could be linked to the process of separation from the parents and again linked to anxieties related to the Oedipus complex. Separation from parents and family tends to bring forward the capacity for independence and the capacity to tolerate frustration. On some occasions, this can, in turn, activate anxieties and stress in the parents. Both parents and adolescents need to develop their capacity to tolerate the sense of loss and to support positive developmental changes. For instance, a patient expressed his anger towards his mother because she did not help her husband to be a better father nor help the patient to cope with the frustration he experienced when father was working and therefore not available. Later on, when he developed a marital relationship, he identified with the negative aspects of his father. Therefore, independence and the capacity to tolerate frustration are necessary qualities in the adolescent that play a significant role later on, when the young person has grown into an adult individual and a partner, and they open the possibility for creativity to develop.

Female identity and adolescence are quite different from male identity and adolescence due to biological differences and family and socio-cultural expectations. As mentioned, parents can also, in their turn, experience a range of pleasures and anxieties, but what is important is that they develop empathy, that is, being able to put themselves in the place of their son or daughter without abandoning their roles as parents, and try to understand how they feel and then maintain a constructive attitude that will help the adolescent in the process of growing up.

Adolescents are in the process of trying to overcome features from early development, both normal and pathological: sometimes a marital connection can be like an airport where they land these aspects of their mental functioning. For some adolescents, young adults, or adults, getting married is a way of growing up and developing maturity—or pretending that they have achieved these goals.

The first stage in the life cycle of marital couples refers to young men and women. In this situation, it is important to explore what attracts them to each other and what the internal and external phantasies and pressures are that bring forward their migration. Why at this particular time? With whom? It is possible that we may be confronted with a complex situation where external and internal pressures are playing a significant role, and positive and negative connections can activate a constructive or destructive development.

Clinical example

This refers to a couple who had reached middle age. Middle age is a particular developmental phase when growing up comes to an end; it manifests itself in significant signs in the body and often in different aspects of life. Eternity disappears, and loss and death become part of life. Looking at past experiences allows us to predict whether each partner will be able to cope with the conflicting aspects of middle age, how their early experiences can contribute to their marital interaction as a couple, and if there is a possibility of creative development.

> Mr and Mrs C were middle-aged: Mrs C was thirty-six years old, and Mr C was forty-two years old. Mrs C came from a country in Central America; her father was a diplomat, and for that reason the family had moved from one country to another and then settled in USA. Her mother was a very good swimmer, who had won several races in her country of origin, and also a good tennis player. Mr C came from Scotland; his father was a doctor and a university professor in his speciality. His parents had split up when he was starting his adolescence. His mother remarried, but he did not get on with his stepfather. His father had died a few years earlier. Mr C was sporty and a very good student and went to Cambridge University where he got a degree. Money was very important to him and he became a businessman, but his business got into difficulties due to the economic crisis in Europe. Mrs C's mother was physically and emotionally very active and available to her daughter, and this supported her identification with her mother. Mr C felt let down by his father, and this made him feel very angry and guilty. He had

difficulties in working through his oedipal anxieties. At one point in the session Mr C said that in order to understand their interaction better, he wanted to highlight their mutual attitude to tennis, which he considers to be a very good example of how they interact. He said: "Both of us play tennis at the local club where we had met for the first time. I like playing singles, and I do not want to show off! I know that I am one of the top players at the club. She only plays doubles, and she is always complaining about her body, her right arm hurts, she has cramps. You can rarely see her playing. She is always socialising." Mrs C reacted angrily: "Is this how you see yourself, and how you see me! You have such a distorted view about tennis and about everything! This is why our relationship is going downhill." I asked her about her tennis. First who taught her and when? She replied: "My mother and before I went to secondary school. I love playing tennis and I am very good! I play doubles, and last year my tennis partner and I won a couple of club tournaments. In addition, I and my doubles partner represented the club when we played against other clubs. Yes, I do suffer from tennis elbow, but I want to avoid surgery. He thinks himself bigger than he is. He only plays on Sundays, and he often complains that he is exhausted because he has so much work to do." In this interaction Mr C described Mrs C as older than she is, physically handicapped; he wanted to disqualify her as a strong woman, while he presented himself as younger than his wife and like a young man or a potent adolescent. We explored how they could make their relationship go from bad to worse, like bad tennis partners, and what they needed to change in order to become good partners—to play doubles in their marital life—what they needed to do differently to bring about a positive development in their individual needs and marital interaction. In the following sessions, oedipal issues about their respective parents came to the fore. Mr C had a long history of unsuccessful couple relationships. It was the opposite with Mrs C. Her first husband had died soon after they were married: he had a heart attack while playing football. There was a significant improvement in their relationship. We discussed their identification with different aspects of their parents and their difficulties of dealing with loss. The following month Mrs C announced that she was pregnant. This was a creative step and I was pleased to witness their interaction as parents.

The next example refers to a married couple who are approaching old age. It is important to acknowledge that in countries where health and economic conditions are very low, adolescence and old age have a very brief span.

When the marital couple steps into old age, this presents a major test to their psychic equilibrium and their capacity to develop. Prior to this phase of the life cycle, growth and development have been an ongoing challenge. Now the big challenge is how to continue growing and developing while physical and mental decline is hovering like a menacing cloud. This cloud foretells the losses to come: social discrimination filters through everyday life, and illness and death become part of the individual's universe. The fear is that the partner could die, or that one partner will die first. The main aim is to avoid confronting the limitations that are developing within the ageing process and the difficulties that these bring with them: retirement, lack of work achievements or losing some of the ability to work, the death of relatives and friends, diminishing physical and intellectual capacities, illness and accidents, and, ultimately, one's own death. To be creative at this stage of life is difficult, but there are many examples of artists developing their creativity when they reach middle age.

Mrs D is sixty-two years old and Mr D is sixty-four years old. In the present session they had a long discussion about their interaction. She complained that he always moans about anything and everything, but she is the one who has to decide everything. He challenged her: "What do you want now? Do you want to have intercourse?" She laughed. Then he added: "I mean some form of intimacy!" She replied: "I am going to have surgery on my back next week! I am in constant pain, and you know that my lower back hurts." (I thought that this interaction was going to escalate dramatically, but, instead, it carried on in their usual flat and familiar way). I said that the reference to Mrs D's surgery was important, and I wondered whether perhaps both are a bit anxious about it. They ignored what I suggested, and they brought forward their familiar, repetitive arguments. They carried on for quite some time without adding anything new; their intensity felt flat. I was worried and concerned about their traumatic situation, feeling that I was failing to make a significant connection. I did notice that in the middle of their arguments there was a reference to a car accident. I suggested that perhaps both were frightened that an accident could happen in relation to Mrs D's surgery. She started to cry, and she said that she had nightmares about it. Then she added that a close friend of theirs had died a couple of months earlier while she was having surgery. It was awful! Her husband looked at her in a tender way, moved his chair closer, and embraced her. "I am also worried, but it will be all right. You are in very good hands. I was concerned about it and went to check with X and Y." This time their interaction felt genuine, and I felt moved. Then they talked about the length of time she will need to be in hospital and the time she will need for a full recovery. Then Mrs D said: "I hope that in the summer I will feel recovered and we can spend some weeks in our house in Avignon, in France. I would like to explore the river." Mr D said, "We have not done it. It will be nice to do it."

As I mentioned, each partner brings his or her own luggage in terms of his or her own personality, identity, and personal history. All the examples above highlight the importance of the couple's early relationship, their relationships with their respective parents, and the way they dealt with their oedipal anxieties in their childhood and adolescence—all aspects that are going to affect the couple's relationship. Some of the marital problems can manifest themselves in different forms or shapes and indicate either a healthy or a disturbed relationship. The creative capacity of each partner depends to a large extent on their courage and their capacity to deal with uncertainty.

For the therapist it is important to define the couple as the patient, even if one or the other partner tries to point out to the therapist that it is the other who is the patient. It is also important to note occasions when the couple's interaction seems very flat. The likelihood is that this is keeping the partners in the same place—one that is safer because it is so familiar and therefore not threatening. This is different from inspiration. Inspiration in a couple requires a degree of integrity and courage while both search for a new experience that could lead to a new meaning. It is the process of allowing the mixture of positive fantasies and the unknown to breathe. Inspiration is not a preformed activity: it implies the capacity to deal with uncertainty, and inhaling, breathing life into one's own mental processes. A therapist should have this internal capacity. As I mentioned, it requires courage, because it is a leap into the unknown. The possibilities are many, but a positive attitude is one that is manifested in the capacity to acknowledge and accept the problems and challenges of life. Each partner has a history—individual, family, culture, dreams—but the present should be a new step or goal and not a repetitive merry-go-round. Being able to envisage a future requires the capacity to deal with uncertainty, which can open the door to creativity. This is a possible aspect of human development or human nature, but I do not think that all its features are entirely clear. At one level, it depends on the particular conscious and unconscious aspects of the mind, and the individuals' intellectual and emotional capacities. At another level, there are family, social, and cultural contexts that can activate positive or negative pressures. Creativity in the marital relationship is a force or strength that strives to give expression to something different and positive. It is a connection with life in a positive way.

CHAPTER FOUR

The Oedipus myth and the Oedipus complex in marital relationships

The Oedipus myth has made invaluable contributions to psychoanalysis. It has captured the emotional interactions that shape not only the emotional development of the individual, but also the way in which that person deals with this new reality in different relationships. Normality and pathology unravel through the complexities of the Oedipus complex. Of course, there have been many enriching contributions—"all the twists and turns in the gradual elaboration which the discovery of the Oedipus complex underwent—since Freud's discovery of it in 1897. The history of this vast literature on the subject ... is in reality coextensive with that of psycho-analysis itself" (Laplanche & Pontalis, 1973, p. 283). Some contributions are concerned with different aspects of the phenomenon, thus highlighting its complexity; others point out divergences relating to different theoretical viewpoints. I will describe the myth and especially focus on the object relations perspective, following Melanie Klein's contributions and those of some of her followers. I will also refer to Sophocles' plays.

The Oedipus myth

From the Oedipus myth, we learn that Laius, King of Thebes, is married to Jocasta, and for many years they do not produce offspring. For this reason, Laius decides to consult the oracle of Delphi, whose response is that when Laius was a young man, while he was teaching a boy to handle a Greek chariot, he abducted the boy from his father. He was teaching the boy to be a man, but he abused the boy. The biological father put a curse on Laius: he would be killed by his own son. This is the beginning of the tragedy. Why Jocasta became pregnant is, incidentally, a significant question, given that her husband wanted to avoid any offspring. In order to escape the prophecy, Laius and Jocasta gave their son to a shepherd, with the injunction that he should be abandoned on the mountain. The shepherd took pity on the child and to save him gave him to a childless couple who were keen to adopt him: King Polybus and Queen Merope. Oedipus brought joy and happiness to them, and they lived as a happy family. At one level we can compare these two sets of parents as representing opposites. As a young man, Oedipus was given the prophecy by the oracle of Delphi that he would kill his father and marry his mother. In order to protect his beloved parents and escape this prophecy, he left the kingdom of Corinth. But destiny was waiting at the "crossroads". The rite of passage led to Laius's death. Oedipus unknowingly killed his father and his servants, but one who escaped brought the sad news to Thebes that their king had been killed.

When Oedipus arrived at the entrance to Thebes, he found the city tyrannised by the Sphinx, who had set a riddle that no one had succeeded in solving, and those who were unable to solve it were killed. The Sphinx asked Oedipus: What animal is it that goes on four feet in the morning, at noon on two, and at night on three? Oedipus replied: "Man, who in childhood crawls on hands and feet, in manhood walks erect, and in old age walks with the aid of stick." The life-cycle perspective, which is present throughout the entire myth, is also highlighted in Oedipus' answer to the riddle of the Sphinx.

The Sphinx was so mortified by the answer that she threw herself from her rock into the valley and died. In gratitude, the city offered the empty throne and its queen to Oedipus. Years of happiness followed, and he became a successful and beloved ruler, until the outbreak of another plague. Sophocles' tragedy starts at this point. The oracle of Delphi is consulted, and the pronouncement is that the city is polluted by the presence of the murderer of Laius. Oedipus promises to find the murderer and end the calamity affecting the city. When confronted with the fact that the man he had killed at the crossroads was Laius, he is not aware that this man was in fact his father; to him, his dear parents are still Queen Merope and King Polybus. The full tragedy unravels when Oedipus learns that the prophecy has been fulfilled. He had killed his father, married his mother, and fathered her four children, who are also his half-brothers and half-sisters. His mother commits suicide. Oedipus blinds himself, goes into exile, and his daughter, Antigone, guides him to Colonus, the place where he is going to die. At one point there is guilt and punishment; at another point in the myth, as in the play, guilt changes and Oedipus asserts that he is not responsible, because he did not know what he was doing.

As Francis Grier (2005) points out, this myth highlights the fact that life is not a paradise: it starts with the conflict of two that cannot be three. From then on, wrong development and tragedy activate the universal tendency to "turn a blind eye" (Steiner, 1993, Ch. 10) as a coping mechanism to avoid conflict.

It was out of this myth that Freud developed the notion of the Oedipus complex, which he held to be the axis of all neurosis. In his letter to Fliess on 15 October 1897, Freud wrote: "But the Greek legend seizes upon a compulsion which everyone recognizes because he senses its existence within himself. Everyone in the audience was once a budding Oedipus in fantasy and each recoils in horror from the dream-fulfilment here transplanted into reality, with the full quantity of repression which separates his infantile state from his present one" (Masson, 1985, p. 272).

Freud's theory of the Oedipus complex deals with the exploration of the sexual development of the individual and his sexual identity, as well as furthering an understanding of the structural model of the mind. Freud postulated the existence of an infantile genital organisation and a phallic phase of development. Later on, he referred to the structure of the mind in terms of id–ego–superego (1923) and formulated the theory that the formation of the superego marks the working through of the Oedipus complex. The child relinquishes his desire for his mother, and under the fear of castration he internalises prohibition and identifies with the superego of the parents.

The Oedipus complex for the boy is associated with the threat of castration. For the boy to overcome the Oedipus complex and achieve a positive identification with the father, he has to deal with his castration complex.

With his penis he wanted to be the partner of his mother. The prohibition against this is expressed in the incest taboo. Freud assigned to castration anxieties the category of primal phantasies, which he considered the main contribution to the individual's personality. From this point of view the phallus is associated with self-image and the boy's narcissism.

How did Freud deal with the Oedipus complex in the girl? Feminist critics have complained about Freud's views. Initially, Freud viewed boys' and girls' sexuality in similar terms. Later on, after he had written *Three Essays on the Theory of Sexuality* (1905), he reached the conclusion that, taking into consideration the anatomical differences between boys and girls, the girl feels deprived of the penis, and the boy has one, thus viewing the little girl as castrated. In 1923 Freud put forward his view that the phallic phase followed the oral and anal phases. Freud considered that castration anxieties were basic phantasies. The anxieties generated by the fear of castration in the boy bring about the possibilities of the resolution of his Oedipus complex, whereas the girl is in the opposite situation. It is the castration complex that initiates her Oedipus complex. As the girl is able to see that she does not have a phallus, she cannot possess her mother. According to this view, the phallus becomes the most important thing. When the girl is able to recognise that her mother does not possess a phallus, she looks down on her mother and does not want to possess her. She has to give up her primal object—the mother—and turn to the father in pursuit of his phallus and the wish for a baby. The difference is that for the boy, the mother remains the primal object. For the girl, the situation is more difficult, because the Oedipus complex is a secondary formation: she has to transfer to the father her attachment to the mother. The boy has wanted to be the partner of his mother, identifying with his father, and in order to deal with the Oedipus complex he has to overcome the castration complex.

In terms of the Oedipus complex and penis envy, according to Freud the familiar socio-cultural view has placed man at the head of the family and as the person who makes decisions and woman in an inferior or difficult position. The girl is presented in this way as quite inferior to the boy. Freud's views have attracted considerable criticism. As early as 1924, Karen Horney (1924) expressed her criticism of Freud's theory of penis envy; she was followed by many feminists who considered that Freud's view placed women in an inferior position. Classical male economy underlines men's power and superior position, and places women, and their maternity, in a dependent, passive position.

Klein's contributions confirmed Freud's initial findings. She noted the identification of children with both parents, and she observed the simple form of the Oedipus complex: the love for one parent and the rivalry and hostility for the other. Later on, she concluded that not only was the Oedipus complex formed earlier than Freud had postulated, but it was present during the oral and anal phases of development. Freud considered the Oedipus complex as marking the beginning of the superego, but for Klein the superego is a composite of many part-objects, aided by the processes of projections and introjections, which start to develop from the beginning of life and arise from the loss of the parents. Therefore, the early Oedipus complex was characterised by early primitive phantasies of an oral, anal, genital nature that gave rise to powerful emotional anxieties. She emphasised above all the phantasy content. Money-Kyrle (1978) claimed that there is innate knowledge, and that therefore object relations—that is, the basic relation to the breast—are present from the beginning of life. This relation then becomes a triangular relationship—that is, an oedipal relationship. He stressed the importance of recognising "the facts of life" as an important step in acknowledging and dealing with reality.

Klein's observations of the analyses of young children have led to some interesting conclusions regarding the development and structure of the mind. Therein her views diverged from those of Freud and his followers. When she developed the concept of the "depressive position", she concluded that it coincided with the Oedipus complex. The pain of the loss of the good object is enormous, and it is related to the attack against the oedipal rival, who is now recognised as a good object, and to the acceptance of the mother who is also the wife and the mother of the other siblings. Britton (1988, p. 29) stressed that "the two situations are inextricably intertwined in such a way that one cannot be resolved without the other: we resolve the Oedipus complex by working through the depressive position and the depressive position by working through the Oedipus complex." At one level, when the child is confronted with the recognition that he or she is not the owner of his or her object and that the parents also have their own relationship, significant emotional work is required in order to acknowledge and be able to cope with this reality. Such recognition implies a work of mourning in order for the rivalry with one parent to be tolerated and worked through; it means dealing with the Oedipus complex, which is also an expression of reaching the depressive position. It is also important to take into consideration Bion's exploration of the Oedipus complex, which highlights the importance of knowledge in relation to love and hate. The two sets of parents represent a universal unconscious structure that is present in the working through of the Oedipus complex.

Consciously and unconsciously, both partners bring their previous emotional experiences to their couple relationship. These have a significant influence on the present situation and on their capacity to negotiate their conflicts. The emphasis is on how the individual had to cope and deal with very early object relations and, subsequently, how the Oedipus complex has been worked through; directly or indirectly, this is going to enhance or undermine their relationship.

It is important to acknowledge that there are different interpretations of the Oedipus myth: some suggest that the tragedy starts with the theme of infanticide—Oedipus is to be abandoned and left to die because his parents want to be together. Other interpretations focus on the theme of parricide: Oedipus is fated to kill his father and to take his mother as his absolute possession. Let us imagine that King Polybus and Queen Merope, the adoptive parents, are the real parents. Following this line of thought, we could assume that at the crossroads Oedipus and King Laius enact in transference their respective conflicts: Oedipus as rival to his father Polybus, and Laius as rival to the young son who threatens to push him from his throne. The crossroads indicates a meeting point, the possibility of real change.

Developmentally, for Oedipus it means a stepping-stone into adulthood; the Oedipus conflict is displaced from its original object and transferred on to a new situation. At this stage Oedipus is not aware that he has killed his father. In other words, he did not know that the man who obstructed his way at the crossroads was the king. Britton (1998, pp. 36–37) has suggested that what he called the "oedipal illusions" are defensive phantasies whose function is to avoid psychic reality. Within the Oedipus myth, he considered that "oedipal illusions" referred to Oedipus on the throne with his wife-mother and surrounded by his court, whose members are turning a blind eye. "Blind eye" is a concept developed by John Steiner (1993). These oedipal illusions can be present in all of us in a transitory way, but when they become a fixed feature of psychic functioning it suggests that the Oedipus complex cannot be worked through.

Let us continue with the myth. When Oedipus marries Jocasta, she is the queen, and, as such, she symbolises a mother figure. Sometimes we can observe that in the choice of partner there is a search for the parent of the opposite sex. For a man or a woman, his or her partner may resemble his mother or her father, or the situation may be the exact opposite: he may marry a woman who is the reverse of his mother, or she may marry a man who is the reverse of his father. The partner that makes this type of connection uses this choice as a defence mechanism and this is a handicap to a healthy and creative development in a marital relationship.

All our relationships are coloured by emotional feelings that belong to past experiences and therefore become transference feelings. In therapy it is important to recognise and acknowledge the quality and the intensity of these emotions and fantasies and facilitate the capacity to work through neurotic fixations to the original object. It is important that the couple can protect, or be helped to protect, their possible positive connection, positive intimacy, and sexuality, and are able to differentiate their attachment or lack of it from their views of their parents.

Each developmental phase is supported by the previous phase or phases, as I have already indicated; the marital phase is a significant one in terms of the Oedipus complex and each partner's anxieties.

For men, there are socio-cultural expectations, and sometimes also expectations coming from the father or mother in terms of work or professional achievements and the choice of future wife. For women, there are also the social and cultural expectations that manifest in relation to the future partner, but biological changes are more noticeable in terms of pregnancy or of menstruation coming to an end. However, women have started to go out to work: this has put pressure on men in terms of their wives' professional or work achievements and the need for the house and the children to be looked after. The way all these external pressures are perceived and dealt with are likely to indicate some active emotional oedipal pressures, and this can activate flexibility or crises.

In summary, we can view the marital relationship as a complex relationship between what is accepted and what is excluded, such as infantile attachments and exclusions in relation to the partners' unconscious phantasies about the early object relations that are manifested in the oedipal situation. When the individual establishes a marital relationship, these aspects are activated and result in either a healthier or a more pathological relationship. It is important to link these aspects to the partner's life cycle, as they can have a different effect and meaning depending on whether the partners are young or have reached older age.

CHAPTER FIVE

Movements and vicissitudes in reconstituted families and intermarriage

M arriages, intermarriages, second marriages, and reconstituted families can be considered, metaphorically speaking, a form of physical and psychological migration that affects everyone involved, including those who are not the main protagonists, such as grandparents, uncles, other relatives, friends. In most cases, there are major interactional and psychic disruptions, where gains, losses, and adjustments test to the limit the strengths of the individual, the couple, and the family.

It is important to bear in mind that marriage and couple relationships have, as a result of social and cultural change, gone through considerable transformation. During the last 100 years, the UK—and London in particular—has seen the settlement of various ethnic groups, which has resulted in a multi-ethnic society. Integration and segregation are both still vital community issues and each can be a source of tension and of problems that affect individuals and various organisations.

The growing number of intermarriages and reconstituted families and the number of problems directly and indirectly associated with them require effective ways of understanding and dealing with them. But it is important to keep in mind that second marriages and reconstituted families are not a new phenomenon in the West.

In past centuries, due to poor provision of health, insalubrious work conditions, and wars, the human lifespan was short, and as a result considerable numbers of young widows and widowers remarried and reconstituted new families.

Well-known fairy tales in their ancient and modern versions make many references to reconstituted families (Bettelheim, 1976). These fairy tales manage to capture in their narratives the deep feelings of children and give vivid accounts of oedipal conflict and sibling rivalry. In *Snow White*, after Snow White's birth her mother, the queen, dies; soon afterwards the king takes another wife, who becomes consumed by jealousy and envy towards her stepdaughter. In *Cinderella*, the stepsisters and stepmother give expression to similar emotions. In fairy tales, the reference to stepmothers and step-siblings acknowledges the existence of these family organisations, but generally they give expression to the basic emotions of the child: the unconscious wishes (loving and hateful ones), splitting, and fears that structure the child's emotional development. Step-siblings and step-parents are usually associated with negative and persecuting emotions, while true siblings and true parents are endowed with what is good and pure.

Our cultural constructions attach different values to our family organisations. The rapid social changes in family and marital organisations, such as divorce, second marriages, intermarriages, and gay couple relationships, lag behind our established cultural patterns and thus promote resistances and conflicts around those issues. Therefore, the good mother versus the bad stepmother or stepsister activates conflicts and resistances that quite often have a resonance and reinforcement in cultural values and social expectations. At times, all this makes it harder for individuals who belong to stepfamilies or intermarriage to overcome their difficulties. I refer to this issue in Chapter One, which addresses the difficulties of dealing with similarities and differences.

In Britain, and in the West at large, the number of remarriages and reconstituted families has increased beyond the imagination of our parents when they were our age. This phenomenon correlates with the increase in the number of divorces. Divorce as a generalised phenomenon belongs to the last three decades. It has spread with incredible rapidity in large cities in the West. Recent USA and UK statistics show that one in three marriages ends in divorce. In the 1950s and early 1960s, children at school felt odd and different and were often stigmatised if their parents were separated or divorced. Nowadays, such children feel that they are in the same situation as many of their classmates. Divorce and reconstituted families are no longer a social oddity or an exclusive phenomenon of famous Hollywood stars.

The institution of marriage and the structure of the family in the West have changed considerably from the traditional, pre-industrial revolution family organisation to the current nuclear family and its various developments. Work and economic changes, divorce, greater mobility, mass-media communication, and a general liberal attitude are some of the important factors associated with changes in the family as an institution. In the past, the family was an effective unit for three or four generations at a time. Compared to our present situation, mobility and changes were slow or minimal, and the family integrated economic, cultural, and religious values.

Today, offspring tend to leave home as soon as they finish secondary school, to live an independent life socially, culturally, and economically. The position of women in society as well as within the family has also changed and continues to change even more dramatically.

Migration is a major phenomenon throughout world history. Migration of diverse ethnic groups brings about changes in the family composition, because through migration people of different ethnic groups come into contact, thus creating and promoting the possibility of inter-marriage. Some of these ethnic groups have different family organisation and values, while some are closer to the traditional pre-industrial revolution type of family. The clashes of values, traditions, and family expectations are a source of considerable individual, marital, and family problems.

In addition to the social dimension, reconstituted families and inter-marriage activate early oedipal anxieties. At times, the intensification of these anxieties is such that one gets the impression that marriages and families, or the individuals within them, are exposed to serious risk of breakdown.

At this point I would like to consider contemporary psychoanalytic ideas that have led to the understanding of the establishment of the oedipal space. For the baby, it entails recognising the existence of the parental couple as separate from himself, and the acknowledgment of their differences. It is this development that allows a mental space to be established in which thinking (which entails the recognition of similarities and differences) can occur. It is these early oedipal anxieties that are reactivated in reconstituted families and intermarriages.

According to the intensity and qualities of these anxieties, the individual will either be better or less well equipped to deal with the current situation.

When individuals from different ethnic groups come together and get married, their disturbing emotions can be experienced and faced without leading to catastrophe if they and their families are able to generate an interactional emotional space that can contain these anxieties.

I will address the issue of couples' vicissitudes primarily from a clinical viewpoint and link them to the various interactional contexts within the family and the community at large. I have decided to discuss intermarriage and reconstituted families under the same heading, because I want to highlight some similar psychological and interactional features that are present in any type of couple relationship.

The clinical examples below, which illustrate some of the main difficulties aroused in stepfamilies and in intermarriage, make use of these theoretical views. In one case of a reconstituted family, the parents sought help because there was a serious possibility of the family breaking down. In the examples of intermarriage, the presenting problem was depression in the wife in one family; in the other, the couple felt that their relationship was at a breaking point and that there was a serious threat of physical violence.

Step-family E: Clinical example

Mr E is a forty-three-year-old man; he has been married before and has two daughters brought up by his ex-wife. They separated in a very amicable way. He married Mrs E over a year ago. She comes from Italy and came to this country and married an English man who had been married before. They had a daughter aged seven and two sons, aged nine and thirteen years old. Her separation and divorce two and a half years earlier had been very acrimonious.

In the session I am about to describe, I was expecting Mr E and his wife. This was to be our fourth meeting. I had already seen them once together as a whole family.

To my surprise, he walked in on his own. The following thoughts came to me:

1. Mrs E had a difficult session last time when she was confronting losses and changes. She cried profusely when she confronted

how difficult she has found it to make choices, now, in her present situation, and throughout her life. I remembered that she said in that session: "I complied with everybody's expectations. The same happened at school. Maybe that was the reason why I was always a good student!"

2. Perhaps the husband wanted to come on his own in order to have a space for himself and for his grievances.
3. Perhaps there was a major crisis between them, and he had left the family.

He probably noted my reaction of surprise when he walked in and quickly apologised for his wife's absence. Lucy, her eldest daughter, was not well. He explained that in fact he had asked his wife earlier if she was going to come to their session and she had said yes. But at the last moment she told him to go on his own, as she was staying with Lucy. He guessed that probably she had felt guilty, as she had been out working the whole day and hadn't seen Lucy, who was in bed feeling poorly. Susie had missed school and wanted her mother's attention. During the session he spoke of how distressed his wife had felt after the previous session. They had had a major bust-up. He is quite aware that she is in a difficult situation, but he doesn't know how to help her and how to handle his own emotions. In the middle of their crisis, he thought: "That's it! I quit, and we should go our separate ways! Her children are not my children, I don't love them, I am not their father and they are continuously disrespectful to me." He was keen to explain what had happened the other day: "I walked in from work and greeted them in a nice manner. It seemed as if they had gone deaf and blind. I didn't exist. I needed to have some peace and quiet. I also needed to type a couple of letters. The music was so loud that you could hear it from every single corner of the house. The two boys were playing games on the computer. I said hello, and I was ignored; I said hello three times. When I asked if they heard me, Bob said 'yes' in such a dismissive way that I literally had to go out for a walk to cool down. I am tired of this constant struggle. I can tell them, once, twice, I can tell them off, I can yell at them, but I don't want to do that. Why should I? I am not the mother, nor the father. They have a father. When my wife comes home, if I wanted to tell her what has happened, it would not work, because I would be seeing myself like another child, complaining and trying to get her attention and support, or I would be putting her against the wall." He sounded genuine and desperate when he said: "I love her and she loves me, but I don't see a solution. I know that their father wants them with him, and to tell you the truth, I would be immensely happy if this were to happen. But I know that this is not going to happen, but if it were, it still would not work. My wife would feel so distraught that she would collapse with depression."

This clinical vignette illustrates some of the difficulties facing this family and many reconstituted families. The husband, in this case, feels an outsider, like an appendix, an almost redundant organ in the body. In relation to his new wife, his role is clearly defined, but in relation to the children it is not. Some therapists would tend to pay attention to the difficulties: the children having to accept Mr E in the family as a stepfather, and the painful experience of seeing their parents split up. Others would try to spot the mixed messages the wife gives to her husband regarding her children, or would explore how the exacerbated oedipal conflicts aroused by the presence of a new step-parent affect each member, as well as the family as a whole. I do not disagree with these views—quite the opposite—but I think that it is fundamental to address the notion that there was a pre-existing family structure. Often reconstituted families behave like a family that has migrated to a new country but find it very painful and difficult to work through losses and what did not work.

In some situations, I have encouraged family members to recognise the characteristics of the old family in terms of the positive and the negative aspects. The new family, including the new step-parent, has to be part of this, to participate in the process of recognition and mourning. It is also quite important to recognise which difficulties belong to the past, and which are linked to reconstitution of the new family or their ethnic differences. In my view, this is an essential step if there is going to be a historical continuity in the process of transformation and a solid ground for new departures.

Returning now to the case of the "E" family:

Later on in the session, Mr E described how he was a bit of a perfectionist and wanted things tidy. He couldn't help it. The other day, they had had an argument around this issue; he had complained because Mrs E pinned some pictures on the wall carelessly, not in line. She could have asked him to do it, as she knows he minds about these things. Maybe other people don't mind. At the same time, he went on and on complaining about the children's lack of concern, lack of responsibility, they were not attentive, etc., etc.

I said that I had the impression that he had invited me to see his demands for perfection and tidiness as an expression of his domineering character, or to see his wife's children as a pair of untamed monsters. Either I would side with him against the children, or I would be critical of him. He agreed.

I suggested that his need for tidiness and keeping things in line were his attempts to control his emotional chaos and despair, because his new family was like a boat in a rough sea without anybody at the helm, and no one knew who the captain was. Almost crying, he said, "Yes! Yes! That is how I feel. I despair, and I don't know what to do, and I can't go on in this state. So many times have I said, 'That's it', but I don't want to leave ... When I feel so frustrated and angry, I have to take myself off, go out for hours. I feel tempted to reconnect with old friends and go back to my old life. But then I see a little sign of something better, and I feel hopeful. Maybe I am deluding myself. I try hard to be patient and to be understanding, but when I feel ignored or have what I consider rude or disrespectful responses, I go back into a vicious circle."

I decided to explore Mr E's relationship to his own father and asked him what his father would say if he were to advise him on this issue. He told me that he didn't know. He had difficulties imagining what his father would say. His father had a steady job, was a civil servant, and he couldn't imagine his father in a rough sea. I asked him if he meant that his father only knew how to navigate in a calm lake.

There is no doubt that Mr E's values and expectations have been shaken. He expects a level of emotional permanence in himself, his wife, and the children, which, at some level of his awareness, he knows is unrealistic. I could see how his unrealistic expectation was supported by his need to identify with his father: always calm, steady, and providing a permanent sense of security.

I challenged Mr E's view of his father by confronting him with a possible alternative view; one that saw his father as a conflict diffuser, an avoider of new situations, and inadequate role-model for his son in his attempt to face the turmoil of emotions in the new complex situation. Becoming a father usually activates developmental emotions that relate to the relationship with the man's own father, in terms of possible identification and oedipal anxieties. Examining all these possibilities added a new dimension to the conflicts he was experiencing, and he had to deal with these in his new reconstituted family. He said: "My parents never argued. My father was admired by everybody around him, including my brother and sisters."

If he tries to speak to his wife, she feels that he is confronting her, and he feels guilty. He fails to be this calm and admired figure. Mrs E also feels guilty in relation to her children, for exposing them to a person who is not their father and for having to make a choice about her own needs, which include adult companionship and sexual needs. She has made it clear to him that if she has to make a choice, the children will come first, and he cannot blame her, because in this situation she is right. The children don't know where they are, and this new family still feels strange and not right to them. They have obliterated from their minds how awful the situation had been between their natural parents. They vaguely remember, but they say that they were taken by surprise by the parents' separation.

Later on in the same session Mr E returned to his feelings of hopelessness regarding the relationship with his wife's children. He justified himself by saying that he was expecting the children to show a basic level of respect, a basic acceptable mood, and a basic degree of tidiness. He said, "I am not asking the impossible, or for any form of perfection. I am asking the minimum."

From the transference point of view I was aware that he considered me the expert, with a capital "E", similarly to the way he described his father. As such, I was supposed to be omniscient, calm, and superior. This view of me suggested a narcissistically omnipotent object with whom he was trying to identify. This replicated how he perceived his father.

> I invited him to consider whether the so-called "minimum requirements" he expects actually put him quite high in the family picture, like a mighty benevolent God, so high that he seems to live in a different world. I was wondering if his "minimum basic requirements" in relation to his wife's children were like the old saying: "Children should be seen and not heard." He laughed and said: "Maybe I am too demanding."

I said that I was wondering whether both the children, for their own reasons, and he, for his own reasons, had failed to adjust to the new family.

He thought for a while and then proceeded to tell me that he had noticed that Lucy has been feeling sad for some time; he suspected that she was having a rough time. He knew that she did not have close friends, and the change of school and a new environment wasn't helping her. I also noticed that her mother had been trying to get her to eat less and more sensibly. He thought that maybe she tries to compensate by overeating.

I affirmed his perception of Lucy and suggested that he may not be experiencing exactly the same rough time that Susie experiences, but he may be able to see some similarities and also some differences in this new environment.

He felt I understood and addressed important and painful issues that allowed him to feel moved and concerned about Susie. He had tried hard to maintain an idealised view of the oedipal situation, which denies the present and past reality.

Adult perceptions of the parental couple and the child have become distorted by early perceptions and projections. The theory of the Oedipus complex allows us to understand the intense emotions aroused in the child when he or she is able to recognise the existence of the parents as a couple separate from the child. It is also important to recognise and explore the reactions of the parents confronted with the child, as this also activates early emotional reactions in the parents. In reconstituted families, these anxieties are reawakened and intensified.

When people decide to get married, they may, as mentioned earlier, be searching, in their choice of partner, for the parent of the opposite sex. A man's new partner may resemble his mother, or he may marry a woman who is the exact opposite of his mother. This neurotic choice functions like a bind. On the one hand, it acts as an incentive that drives the person towards a partner of the opposite sex and enables proximity and a search for togetherness; on the other hand, this type of choice may handicap the emergence of a new and different type of relationship. All our relationships are endowed with transference feelings. What is important is the quality and quantity of these transferences and, above all, the capacity to work through neurotic fixations to the original object.

Western society has, through more flexible family and marital organisations, made it easier for people to be able to move and change, but it also does the opposite: it allows individuals to change their outside situation in order to evade having to deal with internal changes. What matters is the ability that couples develop to deal with the similarities and differences that they perceive in each other.

Children have to deal with step-parent issues in phantasy and reality. A common phantasy and reality is: "These are not my real parents." They have to deal with these phantasies as well as with the concrete reality of the step-parent and the family's complexities, past and present. Step-families and intermarriage activate these emotions with great intensity. At times the failure to resolve these anxieties becomes a great handicap for the successful development of intermarriages and stepfamilies.

We can ask what makes a person marry outside her or his cultural, ethnic, or religious origin: is this part of our present mixed ethnic social and cultural interactions, or is it to get away from an oppressive internal or external situation? Is it a search for something different? Is it a rebellion against the parents?

Ostracism and expulsion followed on from Oedipus' two crimes. Is this what happens to a boy or girl who marries outside the group? Outside the group means foreign. Orthodox Jews often consider that a daughter or son will be rejected or not recognised if they marry a non-Jew. Hindus would react in similar fashion if their offspring were to marry someone from a lower caste. Some white parents would feel stigmatised if their son or daughter were to marry a black partner. The list is enormous and covers all sorts of differences.

Intermarriage is a coming together of two individuals from different ethnic groups, religions, nationalities, social classes and implies leaving what is considered one's own group. Some groups perceive this as a slap in the face: for some it is unbearable treason, for others a minor disappointment; some view it as unavoidable in our present times and in our cosmopolitan society; there are also those who, either for ideological or for other reasons, promote intermarriage.

Western society is associated with individualism, freedom of speech, and liberal attitudes, which find expression in the freedom of choice of partner and the pursuit of "true love"—the romantic notion of love. This varies enormously in other cultures. If we consider this in general terms, a traditional family offers different expectations of love and loyalty. Honour, filial obligations, religious commitment, and cultural traditions are seen as being of paramount importance as family values. Even if some Western families can easily adhere to some of these values, there is less rigour, and the accent is more on the individual.

As therapists, we explore how the couple is dealing with cultural differences, how these differences appeared at the beginning of the relationship, and how they have evolved. This exploration includes the relationship with the therapist. There are cultural aspects that may complement each other and others that stand in opposition to each other. In relation to the partners' personalities, they may feel attracted to each other because they have opposite types of personalities and in this way they hope to develop a complementary type of relationship.

But to limit one's understandings of the marital difficulties to how the couple negotiate their cultural similarities and differences may not be sufficient. The pressures and complexities of these types of marriages require understanding of the various interacting contexts. Marriages are not independent of their members' families and respective cultures: in some the connections may be stronger and openly manifested, in others the effect may be less obvious and the influence more subtle, but it is always present. Sometimes the conflict in these marriages centres on cultural differences, at other times cultural differences may be used as a smoke-screen to avoid other conflicts or painful issues. Emotions only exist and manifest through human relations, and these relations are structured according to cultural norms—norms that may fit some people more than others. Some individuals thrive in certain environments and feel inhibited in others. Also, what may appear in a couple as an unresolved cultural problem may cover up the ongoing problems with their own parents. Antagonistic cultural differences that on the surface activate intense marital conflicts are often fuelled by the couple's own families and respective cultures. Social difference is another source of possible conflict.

Family F: Clinical example

The example of family F illustrates this situation. A married couple who had been married for less than a year were seeking help to avoid a catastrophic outcome—either the end of their marriage, or the eruption of uncontrollable violence. Mr F had a menacing attitude. The atmosphere of impending violence set in during the session, just as a bank of fog sets in along the road. As supervisor, I had to support the therapist, who was a woman and who felt intimidated by the atmosphere of violence.

Mr F comes from Cuba and migrated to the United States when he was young; he had been a sympathiser of those who were against Castro and the left. He was very assertive when he talked. His narrative style showed that he saw everything in terms of black and white, with little in-between. Mrs F comes from Argentina and is white. She worked in the helping professions. She was a left-wing militant and had been to Cuba several times. Both had met in this country when they came to develop further their professional careers and immediately had felt attracted towards each other. Mr F had grown up in an atmosphere of physical violence, in which he was the recipient of violence and was violent towards others. His father was also violent, and his closest emotional attachment in his family was with an uncle. He had distanced himself from his family some years earlier. Mrs F had grown up in a single-parent home: the parents had split up when she was little, and the father had not kept in contact with the family. She was very close to her mother, brother, and sister. Her mother was also a Marxist.

They have been living together for over a year. The first two sessions focused on establishing the way they were going to prevent the escalation of their fights and to contain violence. This was a requisite in order for therapy to be possible, but it was also a way of exploring the couple's capacity to tolerate their anxieties and interactive tensions and to change. The sessions unravelled with the exploration of their cultural differences and expectations.

An issue cropped up that was threatening to erupt into violence.

Mr F had seen Mrs F talking to a black man in the street in a very friendly way—in fact he was her colleague and a friend. Mr F became very jealous and insecure. Waving his finger at the therapist, he asserted that he was going to make that man and his wife respect him.

The therapist challenged him and asked him why that view was so threatening and disrespectful. His response was to talk about the fact that the man was black. "Maybe I am a racist," he said. His wife, in a broken voice, said that she disliked his racist behaviour. She broke down crying: she hates that side of him. She is thirty-two years old and wants to have children, but she can't have children with a racist.

The therapist asked what was going to stop the threat of violence.

Mr F replied that Mrs F had to stop being a friend to that man because it was a threat to his honour; it showed that she didn't respect him. He wouldn't be able to control himself, and he didn't want to go to prison for fifteen years for something that wasn't worth it. He insisted that he was a clean man, his morals and behaviour were clean and he wasn't unfaithful.

Later on in the session, exploring these areas of conflict, it emerged that Mr F had been writing some articles against the government of his country that he wanted to get published here and in the United States. "I mentioned it to her, and she went mad." She told him that he couldn't write them because he was going to be her husband, and she likes Cuba, she has many friends there and she supports the left, and she is very pleased that the government has managed to survive many negative waves and criticisms. So he stopped writing them.

The therapist asked Mr F why he had stopped writing his articles.

He replied, "Because our relationship is more important and I want to marry her, and she was threatening me with the end of our marriage." So you felt put down by her and blackmailed? "Yes, this is what she tends to do."

At one level, one can see the symmetry of both situations: Mrs F is talking to another man that is a colleague and a friend and Mr F feels betrayed and belittled. She sees the articles he is writing and she also feels betrayed and disqualified. We can also see the opposite: Mrs F identifies with feminist, socialist values and takes a militant stand, while Mr F identifies with male capitalistic values, fuelled by a form of machismo that is part of his culture. When her needy and helpless side emerges, this confirms him as the powerful male who should be respected, honoured, and seen as superior. His object choice—a white woman with socialist values and a feminist stance—is the right challenge for his male narcissistic ego. She is on a similar track to him, because the attraction she experiences lies in his "exotic" culture and in the challenge to the values she upholds. For both of them, justice and respect are very important, but they mean different things depending on their cultural and gender viewpoint. Mr F's need for dependency and for being loved makes him feel vulnerable and small, with his sense of personal and cultural identity shattered. This activates his anger and the need to demand respect and submission from her. When Mrs F shows him her neediness and vulnerability, she is convinced that he will reject her and walk away, as her father did with her mother. This threatens to confirm her fears that she is not worth it and forces her to assert her superiority over him, which is her way of legitimising her demand to be respected by him.

The wish for children that she expressed and he shares with her is already an embryonic space for hope. It is, of course, also a space for further battles that would allow this couple to confront their similarities and differences and perhaps find a new meaning to their relationship and marriage.

Conclusion

The clinical examples illustrate how the language of blame derives its intensity from the lack of a reflective space. Internal and external pressures reinforce and confirm old and pre-existing meanings that cannot breathe in the present situation and prevent a new meaning from emerging.

In the example of the stepfamily, Mr and Mrs E, who were both supported by their own internal worlds and family ideologies, had expected a smooth and easy transition. When this did not happen, they were confronted with the opposite and felt quite desperate. Mr E had the view that the period of adaptation to their new situation should have been free from conflict: calmness, serenity, and security were adjectives he used to describe his father and himself. He expected that the children's difficulties in adaptation should be like gentle waves that would die down naturally. This version is fuelled by his own oedipal anxieties reactivated in the new situation, where he is perceived as the intruder and the outsider. The strong message he receives is: "You don't belong here!" and he feels ignored. The children found Mr E to be an appropriate recipient for their projections, especially their resentment and guilt related to the failure of their natural parents' marriage.

For the new stepfamily to have a solid foundation, the new couple needs to facilitate an emotional space for the different experiences associated to the past that will allow the new experience to breathe. This is very important if the new family is to be able to mourn the loss of the old family and to celebrate the possibilities of the new one.

When a family manages to retain a sense of unity and survival but fails to create in their interaction with each other the conditions that allow growth and development, it activates what I describe as an "alienated family container". In the case of Mr and Mrs F, when the intensity of their arguments is fuelled by a hostile social environment, adverse personal family history, and intense projective identification between them, racism becomes a central ingredient of their interaction.

I have tried to illustrate the difficulties that confront intermarriages and reconstituted families and the consequences that arise when these problems are overlooked. At the same time, it is important to bear in mind that these types of family organisation experience a web of emotional pulls that at times are so complex and noisy that we as professionals have a tendency to turn into pathology what is part of the "normal" struggle of living.

CHAPTER SIX

Abuse in marital relationships and domestic violence

Abuse and domestic violence are manifestations of destructive aggression and are activated by different types of frustrations. Aggression is a characteristic of our condition as human beings, and therefore this is part of life. Frustration, aggression, and violence are present in the history of humanity, as are love and hate. The capacity to repair, integrate, and be constructive is also part of our human nature. These aspects manifest in groups, institutions, and society in general. Here I will concentrate on the individual and his domestic relationship. When we refer to abuse and domestic violence in marital relations, we include different types of aggressive behaviour that may manifest as physical, sexual, emotional, or financial or as a mixture of these, and women are quite often the victims. There is an enormous amount of research in this area in many different contexts, and its results differ in considerable ways. Partly this happens because there are different types of violence and partly because in each different context violence is dealt with in a different way. The way the law, police, a medical doctor, a family therapist, etc. understand and deal with violence varies. The example of women as victims and as perpetrators comes to mind. The general view is that many more women than men are victims and we know that there are significant and diverse norms and different behaviours in men and women. Culture and ethnicity also play a significant role: for instance, violence inside and outside the family is going to be seen in a very different way in different cultures and in different ethnic communities.

When individuals find it difficult to tolerate their ambivalence and omnipotence, then frustration, anger, and hate are likely to take over, and the toxic effect can manifest itself inside or outside. Along these lines, violence is an outburst and the emotions in most of the cases cannot be contained. Another expression of violence is associated to the need for control or the need for power.

In general, domestic violence in intimate relations is fuelled by frustration, anger, and hate, but on some occasions may be fuelled by the need for power and control. Aggressors and victims can react in many different ways and violence can be originated and maintained by multiple combined sources. Domestic violence in families quite often suggests a very close emotional relation among family members and this tends to have a devastating effect. There is always a reason and one or many predisposing factors. These can be in the present and in the past or both and they will, of course, affect the future. In the past, there has been a tendency to keep domestic violence as secret as possible. Nowadays, the social attitude tends to be to encourage disclosure, generating relevant discussions and possible therapeutic solutions. The present awareness is that domestic violence is a widespread and a serious problem: it requires assessment of who the violent one is, who the victim, what type of violence it is, at what frequency, and what type of injuries there are.

Television programmes, films, computer games, newspapers constantly show or transmit all types of abuse and violence, and many films portray a considerable amount of sex or violence or a mixture of both. To be successful, a newspaper must have a dose of sensationalism, and this includes dealing with sexual abuse and various types of violence among other significant issues. This then becomes the model of identification for children and adolescents. From this point of view, we can say that to some extent sex and violence are an important part of consumer society.

Michelle Foucault (1992) stressed that when violence is an expression of the power to rule, it undermines the sense of dignity and freedom. There are significant differences within degrees of violence. An important distinction is between two types of situation: the first, when the other person is still able to react, and the second, when the possibilities of reaction are curtailed, as happens in situations of torture, imprisonment, and misery.

The way violence manifests itself in couples and families resembles in many aspects some forms of dictatorship. But when I say dictatorship, you may not know exactly what I mean, because there are many different types of dictatorships. There are certain characteristics that are common to all of them, but there are also significant variations between dictatorships. What characterises most dictatorships is power, lack of tolerance, rigid views, rigid control, propaganda enhancing their values, fear, and an absolute view of what is right and what is wrong. In terms of differences, the dictatorship of Stalin in Russia was not the same as Hitler's in Germany, Tito's in Yugoslavia, Idi Amin's in Uganda, Saddam Hussein's in Iraq, or the military dictatorship in Argentina.

The same could be said of couples and families: when any form of violence is placed at the service of domination and rule, there will be significant differences between them. Violence is associated with the notion of power whereby an individual, group, or institution exercises violence against another group, whether it is physical, psychic, or social violence. In relation to the latter, the most common is economic violence. The power that fuels the violence is maintained by a situation of inequality and injustice through individual, family, or social interactions. The patriarchal organisation of our culture has for generations given rise to many forms of abuse. It is women, children, and the elderly who have traditionally been more at risk. But violence can also be the expression of weakness and fear. Aggression against the other is an act that damages or intends to affect the rights of the other person at a physical, emotional, economic, or socio-cultural level. It refers to feelings of anger or hatred that may get channelled into action. Aggression can also become sexualised or perverted.

In recent decades, the subject of violence has received increasing attention among professionals from different fields. There is an increasing trend to combine efforts to understand the causes of violence and to find more effective ways of dealing with it. Violence is probably as old as humankind, and the new cybernetic revolution and its transformation of our channels of communication certainly are making us more aware of the presence of violence in our society. As I have already mentioned, there are various types of disciplines that understand, research, and try to deal with the phenomenon of violence from within their respective positions.

I follow a psychodynamic and systemic approach. From an object relations point of view we know that love and anger are the basic primary experiences of every baby. How the mother and the baby will deal with these basic conflicts will have a significant effect on the individual's development in terms of how he or she will deal with internal and external relationships. At the same time, there are significant differences within the life cycle. Violence in a child is different from violence in an adolescent, an adult, an elderly person; there are also significant differences between violence on the part of men and on the part of women. Frustrations and gratifications in life contribute to psychological development. From this point of view, it is important to cope and deal with ambivalence, where both antagonistic emotional experiences are present. A person may react with aggression either on sporadic occasions or frequently. Violence can be intense or mitigated. People can become aggressive without provocation, with minimal provocation, or with blatant provocation. A person can react with aggression for no logical or apparent reason. Aggression can manifest itself against oneself as a form of masochism or against the other as a form of sadism. Aggression and violence can be used against another person who becomes a scapegoat.

There are situations, such as particular subjects or issues, that are likely to provoke aggression. Aggression can be a way of life for an individual, a couple, family, group, or community, or it can be an absence that is present as a threat—like a threatening shadow that constantly persecutes the victim. When aggression or hatred gets channelled into action, usually the aim is to cause harm or destruction. Examples of such negative aims are to intimidate, subjugate, cause damage, to manipulate another person, people, animals, or the environment. However, there is also aggression with a positive aim, such as self-preservation or the defence of others.

Arthur Hyatt Williams (1998) draws a very useful distinction between what is psychically digestible and what is indigestible:

> The basic rule is what cannot psychically be digested, that is, worked through to recovery by detoxification, persists in the form of an *identification*. This is as Freud (1917) stated in relationship to healthy mourning leading to recovery and pathological

mourning leading to an identification with the lost, but not relinquished, object. It applies to intrapsychic fantasy situations as well as to those enacted in concrete external reality ... What happens in those cases in which the psychically indigestible experience cannot be detoxicated inside the self and help is either not sought or is not available? Inside the self there exists the identification with the aggressor, that is, with the person who inflicted the original (or subsequent) violent experience. (Williams, 1998, pp. 86–89, original emphasis)

Williams' comments indicate that the escalation of aggression into violence suggests that the psychical experience cannot be digested. He also suggests that this can be due to many causes, but a familiar one is the identification with the person that caused the original trauma or violence.

After violent behaviour, the person may experience shame, guilt, remorse, excitement, and detachment or may react with denial. Sometimes, fantasies and daydreams become a form of containment against the outburst of violence. On other occasions, it may become an important step in the escalation that leads to the violent action. All this is very relevant to our subject of marital and couple relations.

Domestic violence

Marital violence is usually called domestic violence. It refers to a violent physical or emotional action, which manifests itself in various forms of abuse: physical, emotional, sexual, intimidation, blackmail, financial, social or family isolation, or imprisonment. These forms can appear mixed. Basically, it is an abuse of power and control over one or various persons by one or various persons within the context of intimate marital or family relationships. As I have mentioned, it is usually the man who is the abuser. Even if this is not the case, in general there is gender inequality in relation to physical violence; at the same time it is important to take into consideration the complexity of possible stressors at the individual, family, and social level that can activate this violent situation.

From the socio-cultural point of view, the "macho" man is expected to be stronger or more powerful than women, and therefore he is not expected to be dependent, weak, afraid, or needing protection—all these aspects belong to women. When the "macho" man does not fulfil these expectations, he becomes anxious and vulnerable, and one of the reactions may be violence against the woman partner. Occasionally, physical violence may develop the other way round but is then kept secret because men may feel threatened and they could be ridiculed if this comes into the open. Violence may also happen in male homosexual or lesbian relationships, and again usually it is kept out of sight.

When women need to be heard and supported and their needs are not fulfilled because of their own emotional difficulties or because they are the victims of domestic violence, their self-esteem usually collapses and they tend to become depressed. Sometimes women remain in the relationship; they do not leave for many possible reasons, which may be emotional, material, or social. They may experience different types of fear and insecurity, as may any children they have. The possibilities for the development of domestic violence are many. Men, in general, may find it difficult to refrain from violence for many different reasons: insecurity, power, addiction, among others. The effect of the partners' early relationships and the way they work through their oedipal anxieties are going to have a significant effect on how they cope with later pressures in life, especially during adolescence and then when they move into a couple relationship. Domestic violence is not accepted by any religious or social community; nevertheless, there are different views or attitudes among all these groups that influence marital partners' attitudes. Domestic violence can manifest itself inside the home, maintaining a degree of privacy, or outside in front of other people. Sometimes the exposure is the most painful experience for the victim. Often, it is the opposite: the victimiser needs to keep the abuse out of sight.

In the middle of writing this chapter, I had to stop and go to the bank. As I was walking along a crowded street, I was pushed aside by a tall black man. He was probably in his early thirties, physically very strong, and he was swearing and pushing at a white woman. She looked very distressed and was crying; as she was trying to walk away he carried on swearing at her. I felt concerned about her, as I imagined that he had hurt her physically, in addition to the verbal abuse. As I was asking her whether she needed help, he walked back, pushed me, and then swore at me. I suggested that he should calm down. He carried on, now swearing both at me and at her. Then I was taken by surprise, because she walked towards him and tried to embrace him, crying. Desperately she begged: "Don't leave me!" … "Don't leave me!" I decided to mention this example because it highlights violence and suggests the complexity and complementarities of couple relationships.

As I have already mentioned, there are several models to help us to understand the causes of marital domestic violence. The psychoanalytic model is one of them and focuses on the significant unconscious and conscious processes that activate this type of behaviour. Sometimes, the marital relationship offers a convenient situation in which it is possible to avoid or escape from unresolved rivalries with parents and siblings, delaying the significant anxieties and unresolved early emotional difficulties that reappear within the marital relationship. However, sometimes, the relationship can allow the gradual maturation and working through of those earlier conflicts.

Some partners have intense dependency needs that make them quite vulnerable; they demand containment for their anxieties, and if they are not satisfied, destructiveness takes over. They may project their needs and then, in an omnipotent way, control and tyrannise their partner. Some violent partners may feel terrified of their own reactions; others may turn a blind eye; the possibilities are many. When such couples are in marital therapy, it is very important for the therapist to become aware of the different projections and to evaluate each partner's capacity to recognise them and work with them. This insight, and their ability to take responsibility and work with it, can increase the possibilities for both partners to establish a positive and constructive marital relationship.

As I have mentioned in other chapters, the systemic approach has moved away from the lineal model, based on cause and effect. In the systemic model there is the notion of mutual causality or mutual influence, where all the parts, in this case the different members of the couple or of the family, are connected or interconnected; within this context the changes should take place in the present, aiming at further changes in the future. Following this model, the usual view is that the presenting symptom is maintained and supported by the system, and the system is maintained by the presenting symptom. It is important to underline the complexities of the interactive components in order to achieve a change in the pattern of interaction. Some systems, described as rigid, resist any possible change and it is important to understand why this is so. Other systems are quite flexible, and the members of that system or subsystem are eager to explore different ways of interacting. In relation to domestic violence, these issues are especially important given the danger that violence poses and the possibility of further escalation. An important therapeutic aspect is to put a stop to the violence; another is to explore the possible function of the domestic violence.

We are aware that women usually are the victims of domestic violence, but it is not always the case. If the couple have children, they may try to protect their mother. The children themselves can be physically abused, and if they witness disturbing violence at home they are seriously affected.

Domestic violence can be influenced by the following:

a. past experience of violence: along these lines we can say that violence stimulates violence;
b. narcissistic wounds;
c. sexual abuse;
d. constitutional factors;
e. early emotional experiences that disturbed emotional development;
f. family violence;
g. money or financial issues;
h. cultural and ethnic factors;
i. social situations, including socio-cultural-economic and religious aspects.

Domestic violence is often associated with the following factors:

a. low self-esteem;
b. pathological narcissism;
c. disturbed personality, with strong sadistic or masochistic components;
d. alcoholism;
e. drug abuse;
f. history of sexual or physical abuse;
g. jealousy.

The possible strategies are:

a. explore with both partners the possible and practical ways to avoid physical violence;
b. bring the domestic violence into the open by bringing in a third party, in terms of family, friends, or relatives;
c. explore and assess the couple's motivation to have therapy;

d. social control (if it is possible, the therapeutic work should be kept separate from this);
   • partners' separation
   • GP
   • psychiatrist
   • police contact, if there is a need to block the possible dangerous interaction
   • reporting incident to a solicitor if necessary
   • does the victim want to press charges?
e. reassess the possibility of therapy.

Excessive drinking, alcoholism, and drug addiction are often associated with domestic violence. These types of addiction are generally caused by early developmental difficulties; addiction also affects the individuals themselves in terms of their future emotional development and their functioning in social relationships, and it has a very destructive effect on marital relationships in particular.

Alcoholics and drug users tend to avoid taking responsibility for their disturbing behaviour. In general, the alcohol or drug stimulates their omnipotence and magical thinking, resulting in a lack of recognition or respect regarding individual, marital, or family boundaries. The risk factor is considerable. The alcoholic could be a man or a woman: both present disturbed personalities. The possibilities are numerous. A woman may decide to marry an alcoholic partner because of her own unconscious unsatisfied needs; this can exacerbate her partner's problems. Husbands of alcoholic women can become more violent and abusive when faced with the wife's problems.

In these situations one is usually confronted with serious unresolved early object relationships and oedipal difficulties. It is important to explore patterns of interaction while such individuals are in a "dry period". This should be presented in a positive way to help the violent partner support his or her positive side in order to counteract the "alcoholic or drug period".

A family whose consultation I supervised some years ago comes to mind:

> The wife came from South America and had lived in Canada a few years before coming to the UK. On holiday in Mallorca, Spain, she had met an Italian man, who later became her husband.

He followed her home and hoped to develop his professional career in the UK. They decided to live together and when she became pregnant, they got married. At the time of the consultation, the son was three years old. They came for consultation because the marriage was at a breaking point, and there had been physical and verbal abuse on both sides. He was not working and was feeling depressed about it. She had a histrionic way of communicating and gave the impression that she needed to be on stage all the time. There were constant stressful situations and an escalating crisis in their relationship.

Both had disturbed backgrounds. His father had died when he was a young child. He had apparently hoped to have a relationship with his stepfather, but, he said, the stepfather preferred his sister and used to hit him a lot in his early adolescence. Her parents had six children; her father had other relationships and finally walked away, and mother ended up in a psychiatric hospital. In the initial consultation she said, "My time belongs to my son and he wants my entire attention and gets jealous very easily, especially when I go out with my friends; he gets furious."

In relation to this, the husband said: "I am also worried about how this boy is going to grow up with such a mother. I don't have the experience of a good wife." The therapist tried to enquire what view he had of a good wife. He replied that "a good wife was a person who has time for our relationship and also cares about me. I don't get any of this." The therapist enquired whether their relationship was different or better before their son arrived. Both replied that it was the same. The therapist suggested that their son had brought them together and was now pushing them apart. She said: "I cannot stand him." He replied: "When she does her meditations, I can't stand it." I became aware that whenever she attended to her son's needs, he became very jealous, and whenever she spoke to her friends or went out with them, he also had temper tantrums. At one point in the session she said: "He drinks a lot and becomes physically abusive." He angrily replied: "You also drink!" She angrily replied, "You are also physically and verbally abusive." He jumped out of the chair and shouted: "I can't stand this any-more!" As he was leaving, he said, "I am going back to Italy! I can-not stand her!" He slammed the door. We heard that he went back to Italy that week.

The wife continued in individual treatment. In relation to her background, being one of six siblings had made it quite difficult to get her parents' attention. From what she said, I had the impression that the parents had not looked after their children. She seemed to need attention, and no amount of attention was ever enough. She gave me the impression that she seemed to be on stage all the time. In relation to her husband, I noticed his insecurity and weakness, which had activated the physical abuse. She became depressed and was able to make some improvement in terms of been able to empathise with her son's needs and difficulties; she started to learn to look after herself in a more mature way.

There are some important general principles regarding this type of situation:

1. The therapist should make it clear that the violence needs to stop. This requires a clear understanding, and the therapist needs to check that both partners understand and agree.
2. The therapist should also make it clear that she or he is on the side of a constructive and healthier relationship, and is not siding with the victim.
3. The therapist needs to explore the partners' capacities to use therapy, and for that reason it may take a couple of sessions to assess this.

Therapists need to be sensitive to cultural and social backgrounds and to religious beliefs. On some occasions they could make use of these backgrounds to try to prevent the eruption of violence. The negotiation of the above should not give the message that the therapist is on the side of the victim or only interested in treating the eruption and conse-quences of violence.

During this initial process, which may take more than one or two ses-sions, it is necessary to assess the family members' capacity to under-stand and gain insight.

Profile of the perpetuator

a. poor capacity to contain anxiety;
b. poor capacity to express emotions verbally;
c. poor capacity to cope with loss, separation, and feelings of jealousy;

d. omnipotence and intense mechanisms of projective identification;
e. insecurity and paranoid reactions;
f. history of neglect or abuse.

Evaluating risks

a. Have there been previous incidents in the past?
b. What triggered the escalation, and how did the escalation come about?
c. What are the injuries or damage?
d. What can activate a further escalation?
e. Who else is affected?
f. Are there children?
g. Are they at risk?
h. What is the effect on them?
i. What measures need to be put in place to ensure that marital treatment is possible and should continue?

CHAPTER SEVEN

Technique

U nderstanding, exploring, and treating marital relationships is a very complex task. Even defining what is a normal or functioning relationship and what is abnormal or dysfunctional can activate different points of views. It is easier to diagnose abnormalities, illnesses, or dysfunctions than normality or health in individuals, marriages, or families. It is easy to become moralistic. Normality is a relative concept–; there are several approaches and divergent theoretical viewpoints. Marital therapy has developed from a broad and unsophisticated beginning and that it has been influenced by different types of theoretical and technical models. Important aspects to take into consideration are anxieties that are manageable, not psychotic, and a capacity for love and positive constructive attitudes. Even these are complex views that can be affected by different therapeutic theories and social and cultural perspectives.

Marital therapy has mixed and unclear origins, and in spite of the massive changes that families and couples have undergone in the last century due to technological developments, migrations, and socio-cultural changes, it is only in recent decades that marital therapy has acquired a degree of unity and identity as a particular discipline.

I would like to mention, as historical background, that according to the foreword written in 1995 by J. L. Moreno's wife, Zerka Moreno (1995), for *Psychodrama and Systemic Therapy* (Farmer, 1995), Moreno first described his work in a paper in *Sociometry, A Journal of Interpersonal Relation*, in 1937. In this paper he wrote about the work he had done with marital pairs and also made reference to marital triangles. It was also the first time that he made use of the term "auxiliary ego"—referring to the therapist as a go-between in the therapeutic process. However, the work and the book that created a more coherent approach to marital therapy is *Marital Tensions* (Dicks, 1967). This illustrated the marital practice developed at the marital unit of the Tavistock Clinic and the theoretical approach that follows a psychoanalytic perspective, emphasising the importance of the interaction of two individuals with their own respective histories and families at a conscious and unconscious level. Insight is one of the main goals in this type of approach, and past and present affect each other. It is important not to overlook this and to avoid seeing the couple as a form of unity without internal and external links.

The criteria that will decide when to treat a couple, a family, an individual, or a child vary according to the theoretical approach and the understanding of the presenting problem. Sometimes a couple presents a clear marital problem; at other times one partner puts the blame on the other to explain their marital difficulties; on yet other occasions the couple may use the family or their children, if they have any, to hide their marital problem. The main problem can manifest itself in different areas and different contexts.

Marital therapy can take place with one therapist or with two, in which case we are referring to co-therapy. This presents the possibility of there being therapists of different genders, which favours the transference of bonds and phantasies in different ways. It is important that both therapists are able to function in a positive way and explore constructively their different views and their own counter-transference experiences.

When a couple agree to have marital therapy, it is clear that either one or both of them are looking for help. This means achieving a change that either one or both consider positive. What brings a couple to seek help could have many different ingredients, from the personal at a conscious and unconscious level to external pressure coming from their respective families or other external contexts. Quite often, marital couples come for therapeutic help because they feel that stress and conflicts are overloading their coping capacities. Difficulties or symptoms are threatening their relationship; they may even fear that the relationship could break down. Usually one member of the couple will put the blame on the other. If they have children, then the children's problems may be connected to the marital problem—and it may be a problem that the couple resist acknowledging. On other occasions, family therapy can proceed through marital therapy.

As I have mentioned, there are different theoretical perspectives and technical approaches and along these views marital relationships may be seen as a system or subsystem. The marital therapist who follows a systemic approach will focus on the interaction between partners and the effect that this interaction brings to their system and to other systems that are linked to them, and the way different organisations can affect their communications. From this point of view, there are many symmetrical, complementary types of interaction. At the same time, there are significant differences between the various systemic approaches but the emphasis in all of them is on the present and the future. When the therapist joins the couple, this becomes the therapeutic system.

The behaviourist approach puts the emphasis on behaviour and the cognitive process, in terms of learning without considering the symbolic meaning or the unconscious motivation. This view differs from a psychodynamic approach, where the possibilities of gaining insight come from the exploration of the disturbing interaction between the past and the present, leading to taking significant steps to change the present disturbing dysfunctions. The various approaches in marital therapy share, to some extent, the same therapeutic goal, in terms of trying to change the dysfunctional interaction and to develop a more functional or healthier one.

Sometimes, I use systemic techniques or techniques developed in psychodrama, one of which is role playing. First, I want to add a few words about what a role is: a role is a behavioural unit that emerges through a mixture of cultural, social, and family expectations and personal conscious and unconscious emotional experiences and expectations. In marital relations, the partners' respective roles develop through their own personal experiences and expectations and what they expect from the other partner. This includes hidden areas, at a conscious and unconscious level, that connect their roles with their views and possible identifications with their respective fathers or mothers. When I use role play, I try to explore the partners' identifications with their own parental figures, as well as their own views from inside and from outside. This allows an exploration of how they see each other. It is further reinforced by role-playing an exchange of roles and also by making it possible to create new roles, which may lead to a creative development.

In general, the very first step is to consider and try to understand why the couple was referred and what the problem is from the referrer's point of view. The therapist may have a lot of information about the couple and their history before the first contact, but it is important that he or she manages to develop a therapeutic attitude that feels like the exploration of new territory and is able to focus on the "here and now". This means keeping an open mind, with as little preconception as possible, as this can interfere or block the initial therapeutic exploration and assessment.

Usually, one of the members of the couple is keen to start therapy, or to initiate the arrangement to get help. The next step is to take note of what the presenting problem is from *both* partner's point of view. This initial exploratory meeting will allow the possibility of a therapeutic contract.

The therapist is aware that both partners bring into their interactions with each other their own personalities developed through their own past experiences. All this is likely to influence their expectations, hopes, and anxieties. It is important to try to understand their experiences of each other through their patterns of interaction and their possible projections. One possible therapeutic step is to try to communicate to them the understanding we have gained and to observe what they do with it. Do they have a capacity for insight? If the answer is yes, how is this going to affect their pattern of interaction? If the answer is no, then what other strategies can be pursued? The possibilities are numerous and we try to follow them and, at the same time, keep an eye on our own counter-transference as a way of avoiding interference in our capacity to understand and promote therapeutic development. A familiar step to take is to find out from both partners how each of them understands the presenting problem that they have mentioned at the beginning of the interview. A challenging question is to ask both partners what their relationship would be like if the presenting symptom or problem were to be solved, as each partner may have different views about this. This could be followed with an enquiry about what they have already done or tried to do in order to deal with the presenting problem.

At a certain stage in therapy I consider that it is useful to assess or reassess the following, as their views could have changed:

- Why was the couple advised to seek therapeutic help, and who referred them?
- From the marital perspective, who is the one who thinks that they need therapeutic help and why?
- What is the problem?
- Why is there need for help now?
- Did the couple have a good relationship once? Why and when did it stop?
- What type of help and solutions have they tried in the past?
- Does anyone in their family or among their friends, in the past or in the present, have a similar problem?

Following the initial assessment and subsequent questions, as described above, I consider that a possible therapeutic strategy is the exploration of how the marriage has come about. It is then necessary to look at what preformed views each partner and their families held before they got together, and how this relates to their pattern of interaction in the present—in other words, how past views have been affected or changed. If that is the case, I find it useful to explore these issues in relation to present, past, and future. The couple's respective social and cultural contexts, as well as their respective life cycles, are, of course, very important.

Intimacy and sex are important aspects of the marital relationship. Sometimes it is very useful to explore the couple's intimacy and sexual relationship, as this highlights their emotional interactions, in terms of expressing love towards each other, commitment, pleasure, anxieties, rejection, or abuse. The possibilities are many; bringing these interactions within the contexts of time, space, and internal and external boundaries in relation to their initial encounter and the present interaction, is likely to highlight significant features. If there is intimacy in their relationship it could be useful to explore its development, from when it started to how it developed to the present and how they would like it to be in the future. It is also important to compare their intimacy with the couple's views or fantasies of their parents' intimacy. It is relevant to pay attention to the current pattern of interaction, in terms of their communication and miscommunication and their views about their respective roles. All these issues manifest in their interaction and are supported by their conscious and unconscious hopes or expectations and fears.

In relation to the therapeutic praxis, I also consider important the following exploration:

- find out when they met for the first time and who was the first one that felt attracted to the other
- find out if the couple live together; since when?
- determine their present life cycle
- determine when the presenting problem developed
- explore their agreement and their disagreement about it
- why now?
- what could be the benefits if the problem were solved?
- what could be the negative outcome?
- explore how they managed the previous stage of their respective life cycles, and what their expectations are for the next one.

In addition, I consider it important to draw attention to the following:

1. Role-play: this is particularly useful at different levels. It includes the exploration of their views of each other. This should highlight fulfilled and unfulfilled views and expectations of each other and the couple as a unit. It allows the exploration of their roles along their respective life cycles and their expectations, and also is useful to explore their family members' respective roles.
2. Explore mutual projections: a psychoanalytic understanding of object relations and oedipal anxieties is extremely important to discern the partners' projections and relationships, which are coloured by their transference. Their capacity for insight is important in relation to these issues.
3. Circular questioning: this was developed by the Milan Team, which followed a systemic approach. This allows the individual to experience how the other relates to him or her, and vice versa, providing a cognitive and experiential input and furthering the individual's existing view.
4. Underline the existing feature in the couple's interaction and explore its possible meaning, and search for the new meaning they want to achieve: explore their capacity to contain frustration and the

possibility of psychic change. In order to achieve this, there are two preconditions: (a) creation of a therapeutic space to feel, think, and have introspection, and (b) stimulation of curiosity. Therapy without curiosity is a therapy that is crippled.

5. Explore the partners' existing marital identity and what their new marital identity should be, as well as their individual identities and their narcissism. Their capacity to tolerate and respect their individual identities is very important; these identities can be affected through their interaction. The couple need to agree and assert what the marital identity is that would satisfy them.

6. Find a person whom both of them admire because he or she has the emotional capacity and emotional attitude to deal with the existing type of problem. I borrow this technique from eye movement desensitisation and reprocessing (EMDR) and then make use of it through role-playing.

To put forward the various technical approaches in terms of their objectives, rules, and different theoretical views used in the in treatment of couples or marriages is a very complex task, and I do not think that this could be achieved with universal consensus and approval. There is the possibility of choosing or blending different conceptual approaches from different conceptual models—in other words, clinical experience has taught us that there are various possible paths to the expression of a problem, and that there are different ways of understanding and dealing with it.

As I have mentioned, in a broad sense each of the therapeutic approaches aims to develop a better way of dealing with marital difficulties. This could mean improving as a couple, but it is important to be aware that on some occasions a better outcome may lead to separation. Therefore, separation could be the expression of either a destructive interaction or a constructive move.

In relation to this and other issues it is useful to explore the couple's views of what is a good or functional relationship or marriage and what is a dysfunctional or pathological one. In the process of dealing with minor and serious disturbances, anxieties about change may come to the fore. Change can mean progress, but partners and therapists can be obsessed by it. Change can be constructive, but it can also be the opposite. It is important to outline that the couple need to assert what situations or issues they do not want to change because they are positive and valued by them, but when the disturbance or pathology in one of the partners is quite considerable, I keep open the possibility of referring the very disturbed partner for a psychiatric assessment or psychiatric treatment.

The psychodynamic perspective places the focus of exploration on motivations, identifications, and mutual projections as a way of connecting to, understanding, and dealing with the presenting problem and understanding its possible psychic meaning. This may be strongly related to early object relationships or the way early emotional difficulties have affected the working through of the Oedipus complex. All this is reactivated and manifested in the present marital relationship. Therefore, the partners' mutual projections and the transference in the here and now are an important phenomenon to be taken into account. Following this perspective, the marital therapist needs to decide whether the possible insight offered in an interpretation could be heard by both partners and be worked through in a constructive way. The marital therapist's focus is on exploring the way in which the conscious and unconscious aspects of one partner influences the other or forces him or her to behave or respond in a particular way. Sometimes this type of marital interaction is supported by both partners, who may insist on their own views of what is "me" or "mine", separate or detached from the other, without being aware that both of them maintain and support a particular type of interaction. Sometimes one partner uses projective identification in order to get rid of what he or she cannot contain on to the other partner. At one level, there is a degree of vulnerability because those unconscious emotions and phantasies cannot be contained. If the partner is able to contain what has been projected, there is a holding or tolerating experience, otherwise conflicts and crises are going to be reactivated.

At times, feelings of omnipotence, their defence mechanisms, and pathological narcissism block the possibility of constructive insight. We sometimes see this situation in psychoanalytic treatment, when a pseudo-constructive positive insight or change of interaction may produce a symptomatic relief following the therapist's intervention. This manages to produce a breathing space without bringing forward a real or genuine acknowledgment that can lead to a significant change.

A couple's marital problems can be similar to those of other couples: there are general issues, but at the same time there are particular aspects to each couple. The therapist should connect with his or her own style and find a way to communicate with both partners so that the therapeutic intervention can be understood and used. The therapist's curiosity, sensitivity, and creativity should activate a positive attitude in the couple, which will stimulate in them enough courage to bring about a change that will lead to a constructive form of interaction.

Again, I would like to draw attention to a significant metaphor: that of a "crossroads". When the therapist manages to activate a situation where a significant change may be negotiated, we can say that it is like approaching a "crossroads". The couple now have a choice, as the therapeutic input has matured enough to allow a significant change in their patterns of interaction. As a result of the interaction between the couple and the therapist, changes are on the point of taking place. A positive therapeutic interaction can foster changes, but on some occasions it may activate anti-changes. As I mentioned in relation to the negative therapeutic reaction, these anti-changes can be produced by the couple or by either partner, or, on some occasions, by the therapist. It is quite important for the therapist to be able to scrutinise these changes or lack of changes, both in the session and outside therapy, independently of the therapeutic approach or context.

Migration has increased enormously. This has resulted in an increase in the number of ethnically mixed marriages, and this is going to increase even further. We know that in the past this has enriched some marriages and produced serious conflicts in others. I want to make some references at this point to the type of marriage where the partners' personal conflicts are likely to be affected by their ethnic differences, a topic that is discussed in detail in Chapter Five. I want to underline the importance of paying attention to the type of communication and possible meanings established by both partners in their relationship. I consider that their communication is a type of interacting behaviour that can be enriching and therefore positive, but unfortunately we are often confronted with the opposite possibility. In relation to this situation, when there is physical violence, the first step in therapy is to ensure that it should stop. Sometimes the therapeutic intervention can deal with this situation; otherwise external measures need to be used in order to achieve this. In relation to violence, there are different types of violence, as detailed in Chapter Six. Violence can be understood at one level as a form of power or control and also as a significant type of interaction and communication. In some cases the couple's violent behaviour and extreme views of each other can be understood as belonging to a very irrational or primitive domain, which has been described in psychoanalysis and especially by Klein, Rosenfeld, and Bion. These are very entrenched views that characterise patterns of transactions in some couples. It is important to be aware that on some occasions one or both partners try to present as very rational and with a balanced attitude, hiding the hateful and violent behaviour. At times there is a request for help that appears on the surface as important and genuine, but as soon as one explores some crucial issue, a negative reaction is activated.

For instance, a couple that I saw together with another colleague decided to split up as a couple and to stop therapy. We only saw them for a few sessions. We learned that their intimacy aroused frustration and hostility in both of them. Soon we found that our therapeutic exploration and their crisis were too threatening. They had hoped that their couple relationship would provide them with some sort of balance and ensure that their self-image would not change. But it did not work out that way. Our impression was that both partners were hooked into their past. Both had unresolved complex situations between themselves, their individual personalities, and their families of origin. The death of the husband's father had a major impact on both of them. For the wife, it aroused opposite emotions: her father-in-law had been a caring figure, but the sexual abuse she had suffered from her grandfather activated intense negative emotions towards male figures and was used by her to justify or explain difficulties she had in her relationship with men. The husband found it difficult to mourn the death of his idealised father. And there had been other losses and traumatic situations in his early childhood, from which he kept at a distance. The couple were at a crossroads because through marital therapy we had started to approach some of these issues. My colleague and I had the impression that splitting up and interrupting therapy was a defensive manoeuvre, and we had failed to provide a more positive and reassuring outlook to the potential therapeutic work. Stopping and separating had similarities with the alcohol abuse that had brought them together, without them having to open their eyes to the differences between them and the losses they had to deal with. Of course, if they maintained their separation, they would achieve a change, but not a therapeutic one. We felt that both lacked a sense of responsibility to others and to themselves and that they became extremely anxious when we started to ask questions. They were too frightened and felt that therapy could make them lose their balance. We failed to provide them enough containment in terms of a therapeutic sense of safety. Marital therapy for them felt like a crossroads and we felt that we were a bit impatient, because our therapist's tempo perhaps did not respect that of the couple. Therapists should be aware of these issues. We also felt that each of them needed and could benefit from individual therapy, but at that stage they were not interested in this.

As I mentioned earlier, on some occasions I have seen that both partners are keen to show that they are making progress: they may try to show this by openly talking about their presenting problem or marital symptom and asserting that they want to deal with it. In this way, they can indicate both to themselves and to the therapist that they are making use of therapy and are changing. After a while, the therapist is able to realise that nothing has changed, that this is a pseudo-change. Both partners can interact in a flat style that easily activates a sense of boredom. This may be indicative of fear and lack of initiative in one or both partners, and/or of their lack of tolerance to negotiating conflicts. This difficulty may be especially noticeable in their inability to deal with their similarities or differences. It is important to explore the space and time that they allow to their marital relationship and how, in spite of their wish to get help to change their unsatisfactory present marital relation, they need to use it as a defence mechanism. The therapeutic exploration feels too threatening. All this can give further light to the couple's anxieties and what is going on in their minds. It is also important for the therapist to have self-awareness; the therapist should be aware of what is going on in his or her mind. All this has been described by Betty Joseph (1989).

Another manifestation in marital therapy refers to situations when an individual partner or both assert their grievances in a dogmatic way and their emotional grip stands in opposition to a different opinion. This type of attitude tends to tyrannise spouses or family members. Dictatorial views, oppression, omnipotence, idealisation of their own views, and denigration of the other are familiar ingredients. In general, this type of attitude is linked to projection activated by early object relation experiences and difficulties in working through the Oedipus complex. At the same time there are other pressures—links with their families of origin, their culture, and what is going on in society—that can activate or intensify reactions. These are important ingredients that can have a very important effect on the partners' attitudes.

There are many couples whose defence mechanisms manifest themselves in their common intolerance to closeness and to separation. Usually they project their intolerable emotions and phantasies on to outside figures. Their sense of oneness and their sense of otherness are absolute and not tolerated by their narcissism. The great therapeutic challenge is to develop a positive therapeutic relationship that may challenge their claustrophobic anxieties and catastrophic fears, in terms of total abandonment on one side and total fusion on the opposite side. This positive attitude allows a new way of looking at the other partner and it helps them to deal positively with their disagreements and conflicts. It also enables each partner to own his or her autonomous space.

During the therapeutic interaction I also pay special attention to the way the partners talk and how they express their problems. When one or both use general adjectives and refer to the problems or events using words like "always" or "never", I try to bring them into the singular, and then refer to each partner. I also pay attention to their use of particular time and space. When they refer to what she or he does, I ask them to use the pronoun "I".

I also want to repeat that I sometimes use circular questioning or bring in the views of their respective parents, as mentioned earlier. Circular questioning was developed by the systemic school of Milan. This technique reveals information about marital and family functioning and allows the partners to have a direct and indirect view of the other partner's or other close family members' behaviour. A general view is that one would normally expect some arguments, disagreements, or conflicts and moderate stress as part of any functional marital relationship. However, if these arguments, conflicts, and stresses do not meet a basic level of respect and acknowledgment from the other partner, they cannot be negotiated. Then the intensity of these arguments or conflicts is likely to increase, and the couple relationship may enter into a dysfunctional pathological development. The possibilities of this type of interaction are many and depend on the emotional development of both partners and various external pressures that can manifest themselves at a conscious and unconscious level.

As I have already mentioned, the different expectations that bring a couple to seek help can be multiple. There are issues connected with their individual personalities, different social and cultural backgrounds, and external and internal pressures. In addition, the therapist needs to keep the couple's life cycle in mind, because what happens at one stage of the life cycle can be quite different at another stage, and the therapeutic techniques used need to take this into account. In addition, the marital therapist needs to be aware of her or his own age, sexual identity, and ethnicity.

In one of his presentations, Sluzki (1978), in referring to the complexities and difficulties of training therapists, equated it with teaching art. According to him, teaching is a formal activity. I agree with him: you cannot teach art, but you can teach someone to paint, sculpt, or play music; following this analogy, you can teach someone to do marital therapy. The ability and sensitivity of a good teacher may foster and encourage the creative potentials of the student—a point of view that is applicable to any therapeutic activity or form of relation.

It is also important to acknowledge that the moment the therapist starts to treat the couple, he or she become part of the system, and, as Gianfranco Cecchin describes in "Constructing therapeutic possibilities":

> If people are unhappy with their current situation but are, neverthe-
> less, immersed in it, there must be some sort of "fit". This fit does
> not imply "goodness" or value but does indicate a connection. To
> become curious about this connection can be useful in the construc-
> tion of more viable forms of relatedness. Curiosity, as a therapeutic
> stance, provides the opportunity for the construction of *new forms of*
> *action and interpretation.* (Cecchin, 1992, p. 91, my emphasis)

We recognise the importance and significance of marital psychotherapy, in spite of its irregular and difficult development from a theoretical and technical perspective. Marital couples may seek help for many reasons: because of different types of acute or chronic conflicts, or small or serious symptoms, or small or major traumas. As I have already mentioned, the therapeutic approach requires that the therapist see the couple as the patient, even if there is great pressure on seeing just one partner as the patient.

CONCLUSION

I hope that this book will add further to the understanding of marital relations and their vicissitudes. Marital therapy has developed through a wide range of approaches, but it has been strongly influenced by psychoanalysts and family therapists. Some marital therapists tend to follow a psychoanalytic or a systemic approach; others, like me, amalgamate various approaches.

Psychoanalytic knowledge was developed by Freud and his followers as a body of knowledge about the mind and its functions. Family therapy has had a complex historical development, because the presence of grandparents, uncles, nephews, and nieces, and to some extent the community, creates some uncertainties about boundaries. There have been different theoretical approaches that have tried to understand and deal with family problems. The psychoanalytic perspective, and then the systemic perspective, have played a significant part in exploring and treating families.

I have examined various aspects of marital relationships and have underlined that arguments, tension, conflicts, and short periods of unhappiness are part of any marital relationship. If these arguments and differences can be negotiated, then each partner develops what Britton (1989) has described as "the third position" and Morgan and

Ruszczynski (1998) have referred to as the "creative couple", and there is a constructive change, where both partners are able to move to a healthier interaction.

I have also examined important aspects of the marital relationship, especially when the possibility of negotiation is not manageable between partners; at this point we enter the territory of marital vicissitudes and pathology. This can relate to the partners' individual personal problems associated with their psychological development and their marital interaction, or it may relate to sources outside the marriage that have a considerable effect on them. There is a great variety of outside sources—their original families, their values and culture, their socio-cultural background, their ethnicity, their religion, to mention a few. Each of these can contribute to a supportive or antagonistic attitude towards the partners' values.

From the individual psychoanalytic perspective, I use the concept developed by Klein and her followers in terms of paranoid-schizoid mechanisms together with the concept of pathological narcissism as developed by Herbert Rosenfeld (1965). When these manifestations take the upper hand in the marital relationship, it becomes important to explore what belongs to one and what belongs to the other, and how they interact in their marital relation and how they manifest themselves in the "marital dance". In relation to this, it is important to find out what happens when anxieties are very intense and may feel overwhelming and crisis is no longer manageable.

I have also stressed the importance of the life cycle as a context within which to explore marital relationships and understand the couple's presenting symptoms or difficulties. For instance, I have indicated the importance of different stages of the life cycle: the feelings of loss or marital problems in early adulthood are quite different from the feelings of loss of a couple who have reached middle age or old age or from when they started their relationship.

It is also important to explore how, when, and why the couple's symptoms and dysfunctions have developed. I have also explored similarities and differences, as this applies to any couple; this is obviously more noticeable in intermarriages and mixed ethnic marriages. How each partner and how the couple negotiate their similarities and differences is going to affect their capacity to deal with losses and will open the door to developing understanding and the possibility of creativity.

The individual does not exist in isolation; the notion of "I" implies the existence of the other; communication exists in every form and shape. Absence implies that "I" is absent from the "other". Therefore, the existence of each is recognised. When similarities are acknowledged, this can trigger mutual admiration or the opposite. According to the pathology of the partners, this can be contained and negotiated, or it can lead to major marital disturbances. Past, present, and future must enter into the exploration and possible interventions.

I have also drawn attention to the importance of individual emotional development that will manifest itself in different ways in the marital interaction. If the partners describe their relationship as perfect, with no disagreements, no conflicts, then there is a relationship problem, because the wish for an ideal is connected to a pathology that requires the ideal as a defence mechanism. Either they keep a distance, and therefore have a detached relationship, or they are too close, and have a fused relationship. The containing experience in early object relations and subsequent developmental migrations will affect the way partners interact. This is likely to manifest in the way they deal with their intimacy and sexual interaction. When pathology prevails due to pathological narcissism and paranoid-schizoid reactions, this can activate a complementary reaction in the other partner. Another possibility is that the partner can mirror the same type of pathology, or both may project on to the other their different pathologies. The partner can also provide a containing experience. If this is not happening, then the likelihood is that the marital crisis can lead to a break-up of their relationship. As I have already mentioned, the psychodynamic approach focuses on the past and the present, and each affects the other; meaning and motivation are crucial, and the positive therapeutic insight affects the past and the present.

Following the systemic approach, marriage is viewed as a system in its own right, but it can also be viewed as a subsystem. Along these lines I bring forward systemic understanding and interventions in order to achieve some change in the systemic interaction. The different parts of the system affect each other, and therefore it is important to explore how the behaviour of one partner affects the other and how the system is organised in a particular way. Symptoms are also part of this organisation and therefore of this interaction. I have also mentioned the importance of role interaction, role development, and the possibilities of exploring changes in the different roles. The therapist's role is important and requires an understanding of external and internal pressures that can bring forward some form of enactment.

To conclude, in relation to marital relations and their vicissitudes, I have underlined the importance of mutual participation between partners and therapist to support a therapeutic approach. Along this view it is very important to develop in partners and therapists the capacity to acknowledge and deal with limitations and losses. This will facilitate curiosity and the possibility of something new developing. Marriage is a unique structure that is usually supported by, and that affects, the individual, the family, culture, and society. It has been studied by psychoanalysis and other therapeutic approaches, as well as by fields such as anthropology, history, sociology, arts, and so forth. My own view is that when a marital relationship is able to function in a reasonable or healthy way, the partners portray a genuine capacity to help and support each other; they are able to tackle new possibilities, both within their relationship and outside it. This is quite different from maintaining a type of flat routine. There is a mutual respect for their own individualities and individual needs and they are also able to deal with their own social and cultural expectations and pressures in an understanding and supportive way. If all these conditions are present, I do not think that marital therapy is indicated, but if these aspects are achieved in therapy I consider that marital therapy has been effective. If there is a serious danger of suicide or psychotic breakdown then there is a need for psychiatric assessment and the possibility of in-patient treatment.

Marital therapy is making an important contribution to furthering an understanding of marital functions and their vicissitudes and pathological disturbances, and to finding ways of dealing with them in a positive and creative way.

REFERENCES

Asen, E. (1995). *Family Therapy for Everyone*. London: BBC Books.

Bettelheim, B. (1976). The *Uses of Enchantment: The Meaning and Importance of Fairy Tales*. New York: Alfred A. Knopf.

Bion, W. R. (1963). *Elements of Psycho-Analysis*. London: Heinemann.

Bion, W. R. (1970). *Attention and Interpretation*. London: Tavistock.

Britton, R. (1989). The missing link: parental sexuality in the Oedipus complex. In: R. Britton, R. Feldman & E. O'Shaughnessy, *The Oedipus Complex Today: Clinical Implications*. London. Karnac.

Britton, R. (1998). Oedipus in the depressive position. In: *Belief and Imagination: Explorations in Psychoanalysis* (pp. 29–40). London: Routledge.

Britton, R. (2003). *Sex, Death, and the Superego: Experiences in Psychoanalysis*. London: Karnac.

Cecchin, G. (1992). Constructing therapeutic possibilities. In: S. McNamee & K. J. Gergen, *Therapy as Social Construction*. Thousand Oaks, CA: Sage.

Chasseguet-Smirgel, J. (1985). *Creativity and Perversion*. London: Free Association.

Dicks, H. (1967). *Marital Tensions*. London: Routledge & Kegan Paul.

Farmer, C. (1995). *Psychodrama and Systemic Therapy*. London: Karnac.

Fonagy, P., & Target, M. (2003). *Psychoanalytic Theories: Perspectives from Developmental Psychopathology*. London: Whurr.

Foucault, M. (1992). *The Use of Pleasure, Vol. 2*. London: Penguin.

Freud, S. (1905). *Three Essays on the Theory of Sexuality. S. E., 7.* London: Hogarth.

Freud, S. (1917). Mourning and melancholia. *S. E., 14*: 237–258. London: Hogarth.

Freud, S. (1923). *The Ego and the Id. S. E., 19.* London: Hogarth.

Grier, F. (2005). *Introduction.* In: F. Grier (Ed.), *Oedipus and The Couple.* London. Karnac.

Grinberg, L., & Grinberg, R. (1989). *Psychoanalytic Perspectives on Migration and Exile.* New Haven, CT: Yale University Press.

Horney, K. (1924). On the genesis of the castration-complex. *International Journal of Psychoanalysis, 5*: 50–65.

Joseph, B. (1989). Psychic equilibrium and psychic change: In: M. Feldman & E. Spillius (Eds.), *Selected Papers of Betty Joseph.* London. Routledge.

Kernberg, O. F. (1993). The couple's constructive and destructive superego functions. *Journal of the American Psychoanalytic Association, 41*: 653–677.

Klein, M. (1975). *Envy and Gratitude and Other Works.* London: Hogarth Press.

Laplanche, J., & Pontalis, J.-B. (1973). *The Language of Psychoanalysis.* London: Hogarth.

Masson, J. M. (ed.) (1985). *The Complete Letters of Sigmund Freud and Wilhelm Fliess.* Cambridge, MA: Harvard University Press.

McGoldrick, M. (1998). *Re-Visioning Family Therapy.* New York: Guilford Press.

Money-Kyrle, R. E. (1978). *Collected Papers.* Perthshire: Clunie Press.

Moreno, J. L. (1937). Inter-personal therapy and the psychopathology of inter-personal relations. *Sociometry, A Journal of Interpersonal Relations, 1*: 9–76.

Moreno, Z. (1995). Foreword. In: C. Farmer, *Psychodrama and Systemic Therapy.* London: Karnac.

Morgan, M. (2005). Reflective space in the intimate couple relationship. In: F. Grier (Ed.), *Oedipus and the Couple.* London. Karnac.

Morgan, M., & Ruszczynski, S. (1998). Psychotherapy with couples: In search of the creative couple. Talk: Tavistock Marital Studies Institute 50th anniversary conference, 2–3 July.

Pichon-Rivière, E. (1961). Algunas Observaciones sobre la Transferencia en Pacientes Psicóticos. *Revista de Psicoanálisis, 18.*

Pichon-Rivière, E. (1970). *Del Psicoanálisis a la Psicología Social.* Buenos Aires: Galerna.

Puget, J., & Berenstein, I. (1988). *Psicoanálisis de la Pareja Matrimonial.* Buenos Aires: Editorial Paidos.

Rosenfeld, H. (1965). On the psychopathology of narcissism: a clinical approach. In: *Psychotic States* (pp. 169–179). London: Hogarth.

Ruszczynski, S. (2005). Reflective space in the intimate couple relationship: The "marital triangle". In: F. Grier (Ed.), *Oedipus and the Couple* (pp. 31–48). London: Karnac.

Segal, H. (1952). A psychoanalytic approach to aesthetics. In: *The Work of Hannah Segal* (pp. 185–206). London. Jason Aronson, 1981.

Sluzki, C. (1978). Marital therapy from a systemic theory perspective. In: T. J. Paolino & B. S. McCrady (Eds.), *Marriage and Marital Therapy* (Ch. 4). New York: Brunner/Mazel.

Steiner, J. (1993). *Psychic Retreats*. London: Routledge.

Williams, A. H. (1998). *Cruelty, Violence, and Murder: Understanding the Criminal Mind*. London. Karnac.

Winnicott, D. W. (1971). *Playing and Reality*. London: Tavistock.

INDEX

For Product Safety Concerns and Information please contact our EU
representative GPSR@taylorandfrancis.com
Taylor & Francis Verlag GmbH, Kaufingerstraße 24, 80331 München, Germany